The
Undivided
Soul

Cheryl A. Kirk-Duggan

The Undivided Soul

Helping Congregations Connect Body and Spirit

Abingdon Press
Nashville

THE UNDIVIDED SOUL
HELPING CONGREGATIONS CONNECT BODY AND SPIRIT

Library of Congress Cataloging-in-Publication Data

Kirk-Duggan, Cheryl A.
  The undivided soul : helping congregations connect body and spirit / Cheryl A. Kirk-Duggan.
    p. cm.
  ISBN 0-687-07436-3 (alk. paper)
  1. Christian life—Meditations. 2. Spiritual life—Meditations. 3. Liturgies. I. Title.

BV4501.2 .K514 2001
248—dc21

00-046434

01 02 03 04 05 06 07 08 09 10—10 9 8 7 6 5 4 3 2 1

MANUFACTURED IN THE UNITED STATES OF AMERICA

To

My beloved sister, Dedurie Vanessa Kirk:
She fully understands the impact of faith, health,
and spirituality,
as one who champions bone marrow donation

My beloved parents,
the late Rudolph Valentino Kirk and
Naomi Ruth Mosely Kirk:
They lived the intersection of faith, health,
and spirituality
in their love for us three kids
and the rest of our extended community

The gentleman with no arms below his elbows:
He sat with his wife across the aisle from me
on a plane from Atlanta to San Francisco,
exuding profound dignity and quiet grace,
inspiring me to complete this project

My dear friend Faye Morris,
who has journeyed with me
in the birthing of this
volume,
teaching me to see the grotesque depths of pain
and the impact of "woundology" in concert with the gift and
impact of joy,
in deference to happiness

Contents

Prologue 9

Introduction: Use of Text 13

  1. Faith: Wading Through Troubled Waters 17

  2. Faith: Facing Fear, Moving On 34

  3. Faith: Covenant Relationships in Action 53

  4. Physical Health: Our Bodies, Our Temples 73

  5. Emotional Health: Love and Sexuality 94

  6. Spiritual Health: The Integrated Self 115

  7. Spirituality: Looking for a Way Out 135

  8. Spirituality: Looking for a Way into Ourselves 155

  9. Spirituality: EGO (a.k.a. Engaging God Often) 173

10. Wholeness: Faith Integrated with Health and
     Spirituality 192

Prologue

*P*eople, like puzzles, are constructed of individual pieces, which must be correctly assembled if a pleasing wholeness is to result. Yet many times wholeness is not the experience of women, men, and children. As we move deeper into the twenty-first century many of us living during these apocalyptic, eschatological moments are in chaos, disembodied, and frightened. We are often confused and unfocused. Some of us are so bamboozled by technological and scientific advances that disorientation and frenzy have overtaken us, while others of us are clueless as to who we are and why we are on planet Earth. We lack insight into how we can give our love to ourselves, and have even fewer thoughts about how we can give our love to our neighbors.

Too often I see the eyes of students, colleagues, friends, and strangers clouded by rage and sadness. Although anger, fear, and dysfunctionality make superb soap operas and are the fodder for films and television miniseries, there remains a human desire for the sacred, for the connecting with that which is Holy. This book offers a series of meditations, reflections, responsive readings, poems, and prayers of commitment to help faith communities, large and small, make connections in the realm of the sacred. This volume strives to serve as a catalyst for clergy and lay leaders interested in creating holistic ministries of congregations and constituencies who incarnate and embody God in their daily life experiences. To embody

God is to live in harmony with oneself, to live a balanced life with a discerning spirit in the context of one's social, religious, physical, and spiritual environments. To incarnate God is to recognize that all human lives are created in God's blessed image. To embrace God is to respect oneself and the self of others in a way that ultimately leads to community building, solidarity, and social justice. In the quest to help congregations raise their consciousness about these topics this book focuses on three issues and their interrelatedness: *faith, health,* and *spirituality.*

Chapter 1, "Faith: Wading Through Troubled Waters," explores the foundational dimensions of biblical faith and how that faith tempers how we live. "Faith: Facing Fear, Moving On," chapter 2, acknowledges the reality and power of fear as an energy that must be recognized and then addressed as part of human reality. Chapter 3, "Faith: Covenant Relationships in Action," focuses on the possibility of congregational covenantal association as life-giving and spirit-sustaining.

"Physical Health: Our Bodies, Our Temples," chapter 4, examines the physical and mental nature of our bodies, where each individual is sacred and created *Imago Dei.* Consequently, our bodies are then our temples—a directive to treat ourselves as sacred domains. Chapter 5, "Emotional Health: Love and Sexuality," amid agape, closely examines the sensuality and sexuality of human beings toward providing readings and rituals that help us tell the truths about who we are. This chapter helps us relate to our whole selves, transcending the notion that the body is shameful, and move toward an experience that the human body in its many manifestations is beautiful. "Spiritual Health: The Integrated Self," chapter 6, makes an argument for holistic health, balance, and its product, *serenity,* as an experience of life at its best.

Chapter 7, "Spirituality: Looking for a Way Out," offers new ways of exploring options within the community and within the individual toward blessedness and a daily experience of the scared. "Spirituality: Looking for a Way into Ourselves," chapter 8, invites an introspective visit with ourselves as a way to begin healing the hurts within. Chapter 9,

"Spirituality: EGO (a.k.a. Engaging God Often)," examines a life connected daily with the divine, that also allows us to connect with the divine in others. Chapter 10, "Wholeness: Faith Integrated with Health and Spirituality," weaves together themes of faith to suggest invigorating and inspiring models of living in and around a faith community.

Introduction
Use of Text

*T*he reality that human beings are an integrated, simultaneous symphony of needs, wants, activities, and desires—and when poorly integrated those same human beings become schizophrenic, disembodied, and maladjusted—presses us to think carefully about the various linked facets of our humanity. New faith and health consortial programs spurred by the Carter Center in Atlanta and by graduate educational programs in the San Francisco Bay Area, such as the Pacific School of Religion in Berkeley, and the School of Public Health, University of California, Berkeley, have begun to focus on the links between faith and health that concentrate on this growing interest. This book explores issues of faith, health, and spirituality in essay form with meditative poems and commentary, responsive readings, and prayers of commitment. This text is designed primarily for use by leaders of corporate worship, but can also readily be used with small study groups or in retreat settings. For example:

For Worship: Each chapter serves as a catalyst to provoke teaching and learning on the issues of *faith, health,* and *spirituality.* The book design allows a pastor, liturgist, or religious educator to collaborate in planning services for a year. Each chapter has four meditations that include minithematic commentaries, four responsive readings, and four prayers. The commentary and reflection selections that appear in three sections can be used for worship to aid the pastor in developing

13

her or his sermon or as the springboard for a Bible study session prior to the related upcoming worship services. The poems that precede each commentary section can be printed in the church bulletin as a spiritual development resource for the congregation.

The four responsive readings can be used in the related worship services while the reflections that accompany these readings can serve as additional "commentary reflections" or reference material for sermons. The four prayers that follow with their own reflection or commentary can be incorporated into the worship experience during times of confession, general prayer time, or altar call. Also, they can serve as words of renewal during annual celebrations or as a supplement to the vows of newly installed church officers.

The meditations, responsive readings, and prayers are also important tools for churches involved in transitions or interim pastorates. Congregations who are crafting their vision/mission statements and doing self-studies, as well as those churches that have intentionally included Christian education through adult seminar workshops as part of their church program, will find this volume a superb resource. The meditations, for example, can be used to help focus a vision team on the issues, needs, and hopes of its congregation. This work is written for those who are committed to healthy, well-balanced congregants.

For One-day Seminars on Faith, Health, and Spirituality: The morning session can begin with a time of silence where participants reflect on the meditation. This process can be followed by a discussion of the reflections that follow the meditation, with participants sharing their perceptions of faith, spirituality, or health. Following a break, the group might have a session of prayer and praise where they sing and use the responsive reading as a group confession. The leader can guide participants in further thinking through and then writing on faith, health, and spirituality, using the narrative that focuses on the voice of commitment. The one-day program can then close with all participants prayerfully reciting the "Prayer of Commitment."

Although the book is designed as a complete series, the material can be used in various ways. The chapters can be followed in the order presented, or leaders might choose to work through the book by doing one subseries on faith, followed by a subseries on spirituality, then a subseries on health, and repeat the pattern until the study is completed.

Chapter 1

Faith: Wading Through Troubled Waters

Fatigue,
Weariness; diminished
In the grand scheme of things:
God's on our side.
God cares
When friends just can't be found.

God bridges the gaps;
God holds us;
God embraces us amid the abyss;
God will be with us.

*T*he sacredness of life and circumstances in the midst of crises emerges in Paul Simon's song "Bridge Over Troubled Water."[1] Simon echoes the thoughts of personal and communal pain and agony when we are confronted with crises. This reworked version is the song many of us sing. We sing this song because we often forget that we are not alone, that we have an Advocate, a Creator, a Savior, and a Friend. Sometimes we forget that God is with us and that we are called by God as individuals and as the Body of Christ to be the people of God: the church.

The church as the Body of Christ, as collective and individual members of the people of God, is a place of critical care. The church as hospital and hospice is a place of new birth, momentary viruses, minor surgeries, major reconstructions, massive transitions, and movement toward death. Not all patients get better. Both the young and the old die. No hospital or church exists that has not lost a patient to cancer or to sin. By definition, then, the church, as the Body of Christ, is an arena often fraught with crises. In these difficult moments we meet life with a sense of urgency, life at ground zero. By definition, the church must have a willingness to be in the midst of crises. To aid one in crises requires a power like no other: *faith.*

Meditations

Meditation 1

Faith is an unseen
Powerful reality,
A substance of Grace,
And bridge over troubled water.

Faith fuels our hearts,
Strengthens our feebleness,
Celebrates our triumphs, and
Embraces our catastrophes:
If we're open to receive,
Believing in the fullness
Of the moment,
Of God's love for us.

Faith, the gift of belief,
Tool of perseverance,
Avenue of relationships:
Comes from God,
Comes with the cost
Of giving up control.

Faith is a tool, a gift, and an avenue for building relationships and therefore a way of life. These words are easy to speak, yet difficult to sustain. To begin to understand the impetus of biblical faith requires an overview of divine and human faith as depicted in the Hebrew Bible, or Old Testament, and the New Testament. The term *faith* and the state of being faithful in the Hebrew Bible reflect many of the ways that people understand faith. With the term *aman* in the Hebrew Bible, Old Testament faith concerns the idea of certainty or firmness. This denotes a sense of constancy and support, as in pillars of a building (2 Kings 18:16), or the dynamics of healthy parental love: the experience of a "blessed assurance." This *faith* is a conviction of certainty and assurance.

Meditation 2

Faith, the breath of God,
Breathing on me,
A Spirit of blessed assurance.

Faith, the love of God,
Wraps me in the warmth
Of Compassionate Action,
Wiping my every tear,
Caring about my every hurt.

Faith, the serenity of God,
Quietly calming my fears,
Of troubled water.

The word *faith* also pertains to one who is established (Ps. 12:1; Ps. 31:23) and one who is confirmed in belief (2 Sam. 20:19; Ps. 12:1). Faith is a state of being established (2 Sam. 7:16; Isa. 7:9); of being dependable or sure (Num. 12:7; Neh. 9:8); and the site of certainty (Deut. 7:9). Faith also concerns the relationship between belief and being established (Isa. 7:9).

The Psalms—poems, prayers, and songs written by those rife with spiritual faith—have an assurance: the voice of certainty. Whether the Psalm begins with thanksgiving and praise or a complaint and lament, the psalmists knew that even as they uttered their words, God heard them. The experience of the psalmists was lived faith. These Psalms invite us to embrace a lived faith: to take on the certainty of these worshipful, praise, life-giving songs, chants, prayers, and meditations.

We end the Psalms with the English word, *Amen*, which comes from one of the derivatives of the Hebrew *aman*, meaning to support, confirm, uphold; to be established, be faithful; to be certain, to believe in. The derivative *amen*, means verily, truly, amen—an affirmation in response to what was stated.[2] When we end our prayers and songs with *Amen* we affirm that our prayers have been prayed with certainty, that God heard what we said, and that God is already dealing with our concerns. To say *Amen* in a perfunctory way makes a mockery of our prayers, makes our limp gestures a hypocritical act.

Meditation 3

O God,
Your awesomeness
Overwhelms our troubled Spirits.
Sometimes,
We imagine,
We cannot be important to You.

Our insecurities and lack of faith
Make it easy for us to be troubled,
And not believe:
That You
Love and care for us.

Dear God,
Help our prayers to be sincere.
Help us grow,
That We may come
To love ourselves,
as created by You,
in Your Divine Image.

Like faith, the experience of faithfulness has many connotations. In the Hebrew Bible, faith is truth (Isa. 25:1); faith means affirmation in response to what has already been said (Jer. 11:5; Ps. 41:13); faith concerns the act of trusting relative to the measure of individual righteousness and acceptability to God (Deut. 32:20); faith contrasts people with the bad and the false (Prov. 13:7; 14:5); and faith connects faithfulness and fidelity (Hab. 2:4). Such faithfulness has at least ten distinct biblical categories, from a sense of steady firm hands to a focus entirely on the many attributes of God. Faith signifies God's total dependability, God's works and words, and God's impact on the lives of people of faith. Faith and faithfulness also pertain to being nurtured and sustained (Esther 2:20); firm commitment and support (Neh. 9:38); in questioning or doubt (Gen. 18:13; Num. 22:37). Faithfulness celebrates truth, certainty,

God's dependability, words, revelation, salvation, and mercy (Pss. 25:5; 61:7; 91:4; 119:160). In the Hebrew Bible, obedient faithfulness concerns obedience to the Law, referring to what God's future acts concern and how God's people relate to God.

Meditation 4

God's faithfulness emerges:
in all creation,
in all the days of our lives,
in the hopes and possibilities,
in love and peace and community.

God's faithfulness emerges:
in the very possibilities
Of birth and death,
in relationships cast in truth and health,
in the connectedness of life.

God's faithfulness emerges:
In the daily rising and setting of the sun,
In the laughter of children and old folk,
with every new discovery,
with every new dream.

The classic Greek term πιστευο *(pisteuo)*, the verb form usually translated as "I believe, I have faith," concerns trusting and being worthy of trust. This sense of faith was also part of the faith understanding in Judaism; to trust, to believe, related to obey. In the New Testament, faith means to rely on, to trust, to believe, or believe in. With πιστισ *(pistis)*, the noun form meaning "faith," and in modern culture, we often use the term *faith* without its religious connotation. The Christian usage of *pisteuo* and *pistis* pertains to believing God's words. These words may be spoken directly by God through the Law and the prophets or by an angel. Faith means to believe in Jesus (John 2:22; Luke 24:25; Acts 24:14), to obey. Christians are called to faith in the work of Jesus (Acts 3:16), though such faith is not a priority for Paul. In Paul's writings, faith relates to the situation where one is called to have a believing confession in the gospel

(Rom. 15:18; 2 Cor. 10:5). Faith, as hope, concerns trust in God (Heb. 11).

Responsive Readings

Responsive Reading 1

Leader: O God, we thank You for the gift of faith, the opportunity to trust.

People: **We receive these gifts and pray that our faith be lived in action.**

Leader: Help our unbelief, help us be certain in the midst of trouble.

People: **We praise Your faithfulness and pledge to study Your Word and nurture the faith of our children, of our gathered Body of Christ.**

Leader: Joy to this world embraces your many gifts of faith, mercy, and love.

People: **We confess our love for You.**

All: **Your blessings and mercy are great. May we be eternally faithful with You.**

New Testament faith is paradoxical because we are called to have faith, to believe, trust in, or obey that which we cannot see. We are called to trust through our sense of mission and our level of confidence. In the New Testament, such loyal belief may concern a faith that is tested and then demonstrated (1 Peter), or may pertain to witnesses of faith. Sometimes *pistis* is the faith to which one should be faithful. For Christians, faith means to accept the *kerygma,* the proclamation of God's saving work in Christ. *Kerygma* and faith always go together. Preaching faith is a call to believe, the offering of a divine gift of salvation. Living faith is observed by experiencing faith in action. Faith in action is not a way to bargain with God or earn salvation. Faith in action is our call to give to others and give of ourselves because we have faith in God and because God has faith in us.

God's faithfulness, God's *hesed*, is a covenant faith, a faith of loyalty and mercy. Each day of our lives is a day that we are called to a life of faith that does not begin without the gift of a relationship with God. God's covenant faith is our "balm in Gilead," the salve or ointment that makes us heal and comforts us when we are weary, down and out, when difficulty comes, when the innermost parts of our being resonate with pain. Faith is our "bridge over troubled water," when God is with us. How, then, can we live a life of faith, using faith as a garment of hope? To live a life of faith is to embody God, to manifest, to incarnate, to be like God. To celebrate the reality that we are created in God's image, that the very breath we breathe embodies the Holy Spirit, sustains us in a consecrated, holy, powerful way that makes us sacred. Embodied or lived faith is one of the fabrics that make up our garment of salvation and hope.

Responsive Reading 2

Leader: Come, those who thirst for the faithful love and mercy of God.

People: **God thirsts for us and wants to give us cool drinks of faith to sustain us and quench the fires of anger, loneliness, hurt, and pain.**

Leader: Come and experience God's merciful "balm in Gilead," that heals us, that helps us "march on up to Zion," and scales the walls of all life's battles.

People: **We rejoice and are glad in God for the gift of hope in things unseen, for the comfort of love, for new life.**

Leader: Rejoice in thanksgiving and spread the good news, the gospel of peace, incarnated in Jesus, advocated by the Holy Spirit.

People: **We lift our voices in praise and thanksgiving for the eternity, the blessedness, the certainty of God's faithful mercy.**

> *Leader:* We ask now, O God, fix our hearts to receive Your gift of faith, that will bring a new way of seeing, being, and doing in our lives.

> *All:* **Hallelujah, halleluja! Our faith makes us whole.**

We come to understand that "God don't make no junk" when we realize that every human being is blessed and worthy, even when we fall short of perfection. We begin to understand the magnificence of humanity as created by God when we realize that depicting humanity as totally depraved[3] is an idolatrous celebration of sin and an exaltation of evil, a blasphemy. Such blasphemy closes us off from God's grace and blessings. To be human is to claim our blessedness and our sin as part of our living faith. To be human is to know that we are not God, to know faith as the basis of our total, complete, rejuvenating health.

Some of us experience life as fragmentation, a disjointed existential puzzle. We fail to see that every facet of our lives is interconnected. We attempt to put every aspect of our lives in neat, simple, discrete boxes, and when we begin to become ill due to disease, we do not understand. Such fragmentation denies that God created us as total, whole beings. Categorizing ourselves as distinct compartments often comes because we hate ourselves, or part of ourselves, our bodies, our lives, until we feel so detached that we are not really in our bodies. We become disembodied when we lose the connection with our physical, spiritual, emotional, and mental selves—when we lose our connection with God. We cease to feel anything, anymore. We become zombies—the living dead.

When we feel, we often hurt badly so that we must numb those sensations of pain, of feeling. We seek any "bridge over troubled water." To deal with the pain we may abuse our bodies with alcohol, food, cigarettes, drugs, and sex. We may abuse our minds by bombarding ourselves with visual, oral, and aural garbage. We allow physical, verbal, psychological, and emotional abuse to become the norm: anyone can walk all over us, beat us up, or ridicule us. We glory in wearing a placard on our back that says "Please kick me, really hard!" We let others disrespect us, and we disrespect ourselves. We may engage in excess: spending too much, talking too much, eating too much, or sleeping with anything and anyone. Faith says *No!* to abuse. Faith says *Yes!* to healthy love and joy. Faith says *No!* to being a victim. Faith says *Yes!* to being victorious in harmonious community where we can be appreciated for who we are. Faith says *No!* to suffering and pain. Faith says *Yes!* to joy, comfort, and delight in God and grace-filled lives.

Responsive Reading 3

Leader: Blessed God, open up our hearts to feel and be made whole.

People: **O God, You are Shepherd, yet we want so much! We hurt so much and do not realize that because You are, we need not want. For You can give us all we need and much of what we desire.**

Leader: Merciful God, help us know You and grant us the gift of assurance.

People: **Renew our spirit, our bodies, and our minds, and teach us to love ourselves and one another in ways that are pleasing in Your sight.**

Leader: Give us the spirit of joy and temperance as we move about the Earth that You have so graciously provided for us.

People: **Help us celebrate our planet, its majesty and bounty. Help us be good stewards for all that You have provided. Your faithfulness is such a gift.**

All: **In thanksgiving, fix our hearts and bodies and minds, so that we desire to be more like You. Faith calls us to emotional, mental, sexual, physical, spiritual fitness and health.**

Spiritually, faith calls us to an intimate relationship with God on a daily basis, and this intimacy completely informs us as to who we are and what we do. *Mentally,* faith calls us to train and sharpen our minds in a way that honors our God-given gifts for the good of ourselves, our communities, our God. *Emotionally,* faith calls us to admit our sadness, our loneliness, our anger, our lust, and our jealousies in a way that frees us to first confess these sensations as energies and then live with these emotions so that they do not destroy us or others.

Sexually, faith calls us to see sexuality as a gift from God, that God created sex as good—an experience to be held sacred between God-ordained partners as a communion between God and humanity with grace, maturity, and love. *Physically,* faith calls us to treat our bodies as temples of God, given to us by God, to experience life in sacred and healthy ways. A healthy, faithful life calls us to take an inventory of our total health before we can become well and whole.

Experiencing the possibility of well-being and recognizing the call of faith on our total lives are steps toward a healthy spirituality as integrated, loving beings. This life of faith helps us confront, live through, and overcome troubled waters with God's grace. As individuals and communities of faith, we must assess who we are, where we are, where God is calling us to be, and what God is calling us to be. Only after this assessment do we live in faith.

As people of faith we must also do an accounting of our own lives to examine the good and the less than good. We are called to confess. Only after full, true confession are we able to repent and celebrate: celebrate that we are children of God, repent that we have made mistakes that injured others, and acknowledge that others have made mistakes and injured us. Only then do we have the room to ask God to forgive us, to help us forgive ourselves, and to forgive others.

The ability to forgive is the gift of God. In the Hebrew Bible, the words to forgive include: to cover, to bear, to take away guilt, or to pardon. Whereas both God and human beings can bear or take away guilt, only God can cover and pardon. The most common term for forgiveness in the New Testament means to let go or send away. Forgiveness is a process. One gift of forgiveness is our ability, through God's grace, to experience *at-one-ment* with God and our neighbors, wherein the God-human relationship is renewed. In renewal we release the power that persons or situations have over us and let go of the accompanying pain, hurt, guilt, and shame. To forgive is not to forget. To forgive is to ask God for the courage and strength to not let something have a crippling stronghold on our lives. To forgive is to let go so that we can dream and have visions and be open to community support.

Responsive Reading 4

Leader: When troubled waters hinder our faith and cloud our minds, bring us clarity and peace, O Creator; show us the path toward forgiveness.

People: **God, we confess we want to control our lives and are often distressed; give us a spirit of unspeakable joy, even in the midst of crisis and pain.**

Leader: Open our hearts and souls to new possibilities, new ways of being in the world, in a spirit of atonement with You, ourselves, our neighbors.

People: **We worship You, praise You, and honor Your gift of mercy.**

Leader: Help us, Most Merciful One, to lovingly desire forgiveness, serenity, and hope.

People: **Create in us a clean heart, O Gentle Spirit, as we celebrate life.**

All: **Unto Thee we come celebrating Your gifts and healing ways with the desire to be whole people to Your glory, for the good of the whole world. Amen.**

A lived faith is a garment of hope for individuals and a strategy of grace for the church. To have a solid, thriving, loving community we must use faith as a strategy for health and well-being, for healing of our communities, our churches. Sometimes in the life of the church there are experiences that have shattered the church community's lived reality. Much happens in the church: there may be brokenness, a sin-filled crisis with the pastor through betrayal, theft, and/or deceit.

There may be a crisis due to similar sinful behavior by the lay members. If the church is the Body of Christ, then the church always includes gathered sinners and saints. In the best of all possible situations there are checks and balances in place within the realm of personal and communal ethics so that the "I," the "we," and the "they" can work and live together.

In crisis, we must ask: Who are we? What is our mission? What is the nature of the relationship between leaders and followers? How do we learn to listen with faith and discernment? As a community, what evils must be named, examined, transformed, and driven out? Are we willing to go beyond the denial and the blaming to examine the entire situation and to explore our part in the process that caused our pain? Are we willing to be made well and whole? Are we willing to no longer be victims and/or scapegoats? Every day, God invites us to live in present time, to name the evils, to expose them, to evaluate them, to wait prayerfully for God to heal us as we take steps to help heal ourselves, to begin rebuilding.

> *God, grant me the serenity*
> *to accept the things I cannot change,*
> *The courage to change the things I can,*
> *And the wisdom to know the difference.*[4]

We must take seriously Ephesians 6:12, "For we are not contending against flesh and blood, but against the principalities, against the powers, against the world rulers of this present darkness, against the spiritual hosts of wickedness in the heavenly places." We are enticed to hurt others and to hurt ourselves. We are hurt by others. We must take inventory constantly as individuals and as a gathered body. Are we the stumbling blocks to the health of ourselves or to the church? Do we really take things to God in prayer?

Prayers of Commitment

Prayer of Commitment 1

Lord, we come before You in humble spirit and repentant heart. Errors have been made, feelings have been hurt. We are experienc-

ing irreparable harm and great pain. We come to You with a desire for vengeance. We seek to hurt those who have hurt us, our families, our churches, or our world.

God, please deliver us from being victims of our own anger and rage. Help us use this rage to effect change to better ourselves and others. God, help us be open to healing and give us the strength to face pain without being destroyed by its power.

As we come with blessed assurance we ask You to transform our denial into a grace-filled willingness to see, to accept our part in these troubled waters, and to be annointed with Your grace to transform the present and to build toward a healthy future. Amen.

Through faith, Christians believe that Jesus lives, and lives in you and me. We are all called to a radical affirmation—that someone whom we cannot see loves us, cares about us, and speaks to us. Today we are called to a life of faith, but that life cannot begin without the gift of a relationship with God. Just as God's eye is "on the sparrow," our God watches over us. We are able to take all our cares to God in faithful prayer. Only in prayer can the individual or the community face the crisis and move toward change.

In the midst of crisis we wade in the troubled waters, but we must not wade or stand in the mud too long. Sooner or later we must prepare the deceased for burial. The deceased may be a person, an incident, a relationship, or an old habit. Burial involves a complex process of grief—all those phases of disbelief, denial, anger, bargaining, and acceptance. Then we can, in faith, move on.

Prayer of Commitment 2

As we come before Your presence, let us come in a spirit of hope and rejuvenation.

O God, we have known the great pain of destructive, troubled waters that have torn us asunder. We have known torrential anger, jealousy, envy, lust, and guilt. We come ready to know peaceful waters and calm seas; to bury the pain and shock of disbelief.

We come tired of bargaining ineffectively and with pretense. We come willing to state the past and name our pain as we let go of the

*power this past pain has had over us. We release our minds,
bodies, and spirits to experience Your redeeming, saving, grace. In
faith, we receive Your peace, the peace that passes all understanding.*

Often, even when we desire to know peace, to live in present
time, we find that the process is not simple or easy. We think
back to others who have known pain, and get confused like
God's righteous servant Job. The book of Job is clearly a book
about a person in crisis. Job and his friends debate the importance of personal experience as a source of religious insight.
They also talk about the importance and difficulty of solidarity among those who are oppressed. They try to make sense
out of the old, traditional models for God, and they explore the
relationship between human existence and all creation. What a
confusing, fascinating book. Often, our lives seem confusing,
like a perennial Job syndrome.

Like us, Job asks the *why* questions. Why was Job born? Why
was he nursed at his mother's knee? If this is all there is and is
as good as it gets, why isn't Job dead? Why does Job, or any
human, revere, serve, and obey an unjust God? Is it contrary to
some divine plan to relieve suffering? (The late Mother Teresa
thought so and refused to offer pain relief to the terminally ill
in her hospices.) God does not answer Job's questions but
instead starts to talk about the design of the world, the cosmos.

Why does evil exist in a world created by a good, just, and
loving deity? We do ourselves and others a disservice when we
try to rationalize evil by saying that there must be some positive reason for suffering, or claim that it was God's plan or will.
Believers in God have never come up with a complete and sat-
isfactory answer to this problem. This is the question of theod-
icy: that if God is good, just, all-powerful, and loving, why do
bad things happen? Even if we answer that God only permits
evil, is God responsible for what God permits? Why doesn't
God just stop evil from happening?

Some scholars answer by saying that human beings have
free will to make a choice to do bad things and God allows
them that choice. That answer is problematic and does not help
the victims of the Middle Passage, Auschwitz, and the Gulag;

that answer does not make sense to parents whose babies die of leukemia and AIDS. The book of Job never answers the questions of why people suffer but invites us to dialogue with others so that we may experience God and life itself.

Prayer of Commitment 3

Most Holy God, our day has been fraught with difficulty. The lives of myself, my friends, my church have been so painful. Some days it seems as if all the faith, the prayers, and the Bible studies do not make a difference. But then You come to me in a still, small voice, in a song or a poem, and I know You care and I know we are not alone.

Glorious, Loving God, we want the faith of Sarah and Abraham to shore up our weakness. Give us the constancy of Hannah as she prayed for Samuel, so that we can pray for and be there for our children. We pledge to listen well to Your many voices in the world; to celebrate our going through and coming out of troubled waters with renewed strength and hope and vison.

Today, as during the time of Job, people often blame the victim or decide that illness and misfortune are a just punishment from God. Faith gives us another way to listen and the wisdom to offer concrete support and love. We need to talk about all life as God's gift to us, to live in faith. Thus we can talk with our children and among ourselves about our bodies and about sex as a gift from God; about the beauty and the responsibility that comes with sexual intercourse. We do a disservice when we give children bogus names for body parts and talk about the body in shameful whispers. Treating sex as something nasty heightens children's curiosity and makes its pursuit more of an adventure. Rather than "just saying no" to drugs, faithful conversation involves how we desecrate our God-given temples when we poison our bodies through drugs. If we accept that our bodies are temples and holy, then we have an avenue to talk about AIDS/HIV education. We can let ourselves and our churches see HIV/AIDS not as a punishment, but as a disease of the immune system that sometimes results when we do not adequately respect ourselves.

31

Although much of life is a mystery to our limited human understanding, we can work on our attitudes, increase our knowledge, and help influence our communities about those things that we do know and understand. We can be proactive and have good offenses. We can help victims of leukemia by participating in bone marrow drives. We can help children get an education by giving to a college or scholarship fund. We can reinvest in our communities by starting parish investment clubs, by increasing our philanthropic giving, by serving as mentors at church and school, by being extended family to those around us in need. The church once did for people much of what we now expect the government to do. Has the government replaced the church regarding our spiritual needs? To live the faithful life we must take better care of ourselves physically, mentally, emotionally, and spiritually.

We give love to ourselves when we take care of ourselves and develop a theology of the Sabbath. Too often, when we work hard, we have no time to rest or play or listen to others or listen to ourselves. A life of faith calls for a life of joyous imagination, a life filled with "what if" or "let's pretend." Our children know those games well, but often as adults we forget. We need those with prophetic imagination to guide and direct our paths. Then we need to have an adventurous imagination where we will engage ourselves, signifying the theme from the *Star Trek* series, that with God "we can go where we have never gone before." The Gospel of Matthew tells us clearly that a life of faith calls us to be the salt of the earth. The people of God are called to add seasoning, preserving power to the life of the world, the life of the church. This life of faith is not about what happens when we die. God is not an old white, black, or brown man up in heaven writing down everything we do in some accounting ledger. God is with us now, and heaven is an ultimate, intimate relationship with God. Hell is the absence of God, right now. God is our lover, our friend, mother, father, sister, brother, who engages us in a life-affirming relationship.

Prayer of Commitment 4

Beloved God, we want to be in love with You and know Your love of us. We want to be a people of faith, as we sail on, and dance and laugh and praise You. We want to be visionaries with Your dreams. We want to be faithful friends, children, partners, and family.

God, help us build loving, faithful bridges over the many troubled waters of the lives of ourselves and our communties. Help us be the salt that will preserve lost souls; the beacons that will show some lost traveler the way. Gracious God, we affirm that your grace sufficiently meets our needs.

Like a bridge over troubled water, faith will keep us in tune with You, out of unredeemable binds, with You being with us, beside us, carrying us.

Our prayers, like all acts of worship, concern the honor and homage paid to God by those God created in thanksgiving for divine favor and blessings. Everything that has breath in heaven and earth, everything on earth and in the sea, is called on to praise God (Ps. 150). We praise God with song, musical instruments, testimony, dance, and prayer; through inward emotion or outward utterances. Participating in acts of praise builds our relationship with God and girds up many faithful bridges over the troubled waters of our lives. The certainty of these faithful bridges helps us live in present time, knowing that we can make a difference. Such faith helps produce life-enhancing theology or God-talk. We can then celebrate the essential dignity and worth of all life, affirming God's love and the importance of faith in living this life.

---

1. See "Bridge Over Troubled Water" by Paul Simon (New York: Paul Simon Music, 1969).

2. R. Laird Harris, ed., *Theological Wordbook of the Old Testament*, vol. 1 (Chicago: Moody Press, 1980), 51-52.

3. See, for example, Jonathan Edwards, "Sinners in the Hands of an Angry God" (1841), in *American Sermons: Literary Classics of the United States*, ed. Michael Warner (New York: Library of America, 1999), 347-64.

4. "The Serenity Prayer" has been credited to almost every theologian, philosopher, and saint known to humans. The most popular opinion of its authorship favors St. Francis of Assisi, although versions of it have also been attributed to Reinhold Niebuhr and Friedrich Oetinger, among others.

Chapter 2

Faith: Facing Fear, Moving On

Shuddering, lips trembling,
Not knowing day from night.
I look into the mirrors
of my smoky soul.
unclear of who I am;
Not dealing with Whose I am.

Heart palpitations
Mimicking a bass drum.
Not exciting the days of my youth
when I chose to be free—
Drum major and majorettes
Strutted our school colors so proudly;
How I identified!
Found a bit of God,
everywhere.

Oh, how simple that seemed,
How complex,
How conflicted,
I feel right now.
But it is within this confusion
I must be still,
And know God.

I can be still,
And know God,
And know that fear is not
The Boogie man of my childhood,
But the traumatized reality
I bring on myself:

I forgot to trust God.
I forgot that
God is within me.
Would God deny God?

*F*ear is one of those words we either hesitate to use, or we use too much. We experience fear as a sense of sudden danger and an unpleasant, strong emotion caused by anticipation or awareness of evil. Fear is an awareness of jeopardy, malaise, of something going wrong. Fear connotes turmoil, suffering, and insecurity. We regard living through a fearful phase of life as a liability that will result in peril. Fear, however, is not an emotional encounter within a vacuum. Fear is not relegated to persons because of their sociohistorical, racial, sexual, religious, economic, or political lifestyle. Fear is part of being human. Sometimes the only thing to fear is fear itself. Early warning signals of trepidation or danger have saved lives. But the fear that cripples or paralyzes is a pathology. Fear that spurs one to action is life-giving. Fear can inspire faith.

Meditations

Meditation 1

Faith meets fear
In moments of weariness,
As I hold fast to Grace,
Knowing that God unconditionally
Cares for me.

Faith meets fear
When my tears flood
the rivers of my being;
When I'm spiritually bankrupt,
Yet, I stand on God's promises.

Faith meets fear
When all hope seems lost,
Then God sends the joy
And the faith of a small child,
To delight my soul.

Then faith meets fear,
As I remember Jesus' words to us:
"Come to Me with the innocence of a child;
I will calm your fear,
I will give you rest."

Fear is energy that we can learn to use to strengthen our own personal and communal well-being. To be aware of one's own fear means to be conscious of some unsettling force or reality. Fear, an emotional boundary, can be debilitating. When fear overcomes one's healthy, balanced relationships with others and with oneself, it can become pathological. In the biblical sense there are several meanings of fear—fear regarding human experience and fear in concert with one's experience of God.

Psalm 23 signifies a specific Divine-human relationship where the human not only does not want for anything, but has a certainty and experience of comfort. He or she trusts that there is no need to fear evil or harm, for God, the authentic Shepherd, guides, nurtures, and protects. This lack of fear and presence of comfort assures the believer of lifelong safety, abundance, blessing, delight, and satisfaction. The release of fear creates a full, bounteous life. Faith is one path, one process, for helping individuals cope with fear and other emotional and spiritual duress where because of life circumstances joy and hope are lost. Faith is an opportunity to foster a new and regenerative relationship where God is the provider, the one who initiates and gives comfort, and the one who can help put the minds of people to rest (Gen. 50:21); where God delivers humanity from life's moments of exodus and exile toward moments of healing and wholeness (Exod. 14:13). Fear is a genuine response when there is no hope and when people are all alone. The experience of God's deliverance, however, is an outpouring of strength. Deliverance as a process of unfolding moments creates the lived knowledge of being in relationship, in ultimate intimacy with the Divine, the One who will never leave us or forsake us (Deut. 31:7). We can choose to use this energy of fear to thwart or empower our spiritual health and awareness of the gift of salvation. Faith allows us to see fear as a force that can be lived with and overcome in a way that does not destroy our selves or our love for life and humanity. The fear of God, on the other hand, in the biblical sense, is to be embraced from a context of gratitude, worship, and joy.

The fear of God is equated with the beginning of wisdom, the foundation of knowledge (Prov. 1:7), which gives respect for God. In Proverbs, Ecclesiastes, and Job, the Wisdom books of the Hebrew Text, *Wisdom* is a modern critical term that categorizes writing flourishing in ancient Israel and throughout the ancient Near East. Wisdom is a way of life, of understanding the world. For with wisdom, beneath all the apparent injustice, confusion, and disorder apparent in life, there is divine ordering by which one can ultimately understand everything connecting wisdom/prosperity and folly/destruction. In this dual system, when one is wise, one prospers; when one commits folly, one experiences destruction.

Theologically, significant issues are justice, truth, mutuality, consistency, and power. Life makes sense and the order of the universe is meaningful because order, goodness, and meaning is foundational to the world and one can rely on the credibility of one's own experience. This type of order reflects the mind and will of God. Life, entrusted as gift to humanity, is an opportunity for humanity to be responsible. Such a gift of life and the world are to be shared, celebrated, enjoyed—a reality where God is constantly present to support, nurture, and facilitate humanity toward experiencing a holistic life.

Meditation 2

Fear smarts our terror-ladened eyes,
Weary from hopelessness;
Red from tears that refuse to fall;
Holding on to what never was,
Stumbling blocks for what never can be.

When pain and desperation
Paralyze the morning dew of possibilities,
Lost in quagmires of doubt; perhaps shame
We never knew we had;
We never knew we lost.

Fear can be life-defeating,
When the fabric of our lives
Erodes to remnants
Too brittle to be quilted,
into the warm divine connectedness.

37

> *Fear can be life-generating,*
> *Sparking newness,*
> *Of humanness, of loving Godliness,*
> *Of being real.*

Fear of the Lord is a synonym for respecting, for being faithful to God. Living out this faithful respect is a commitment first to listening to God, to obeying God's commandments, and then living out and teaching those commandments to one's children and community. These commandments call for allegiance, devotion, and love for God—a love that then transposes to one's offspring and simultaneously calls to one's ancestors, who were also faithful. To fear God is to love and respect God. Love and respect are the cornerstones for all relationships. Immersed in the love of self, and therefore of God and one's neighbor, is antithetical to being trapped by fear.

FEAR is *F*alse *E*vidence *A*nticipating *R*eality. Fear is faith in false evidence—in the illusion of random hazards and chaos rather than in the reality of divine order. The fear that stings is false evidence appearing real: our anxious thoughts and feelings are so overwhelming that they distort how we perceive reality. This type of energy is a fierce hunger that gnaws at one's being and can cause different human appetites to become addictive behaviors. Such fear skews how an individual can read reality. And if fear serves as the key generative life factor, that fear is dangerous. Fear shaped positively fuels productivity and may manifest itself as passion.

When *FEAR* becomes *F*atal *E*xaggerated *A*ngst *R*ealized the depths of despair may be so great that one becomes ill, depressed, spiritually paralyzed. In such moments God often comes as a still, quiet voice. Then one has to take a leap of faith to begin to trust the possibility that One greater can empower, can restore one to balance, to sanity. The experience of *FEAR*, of *F*eelings *E*lectrically *A*ccelerated *R*eceived, is the experience of intense energy, the energy that we name *fear*, but over which we can exert control. We can live a life where we are not stymied by the particular configuration of energy we call *fear*.

Fear as passion: a desire, an enthusiasm, or an excitement or craving for something else, can drive one to self-destruction.

Fear is a dangerous thing when it goes unchecked. When antici-pating danger, fear triggers panic, dread, fright, or painful agita-tion. Fear can become so all-encompassing that one is paralyzed and can no longer function in daily camaraderie. Fear that has been shaped positively by faith into passion engenders hope. Fear that becomes hope sparks optimistic confidence and allows one to expect miracles. To experience a miracle is to have a childlike wonderment about life, revelation, and the marvels of God all about us. Hope reshapes fear toward conversion and change. An optimistic outlook often helps us transcend victim-hood and denial. When fear is transformed into hope, we grow and have the discipline necessary to help affect change. As redirected emotional energy, transformed **FEAR** becomes *F*requent *E*xceptional *A*wesome *R*everence.

*F*requent *E*xceptional *A*wesome *R*everence is a new way of being, a way to experience God in powerful ways. This experi-ence comes as daily spiritual experiences through moments of revelation, joy, praise, and prayer. This kind of intimacy creates an air of excellence that is beyond the mundane, the arrogant, that which is false and irrelevant. Such daily liturgy is awe-some, amazing, yet grounded in a community of faith with God. That kind of energy sees the *Imago Dei* in all people and reveres the gift of life itself, seeking to connect with that part of humanity in diverse ways. This kind of reshaped fear is a rev-erential awe of God that moves us to be in God's presence, to know God as that which cannot be reduced, that which cares for us profoundly.

Meditation 3

Anxiety prone
I saw the lilies of the field,
Neither sowing, nor reaping,
Surviving still.

I decided to remove the shackles of guilt,
The ropes of disgust,
The chains of not good enough,
The prisons of doubt:
I felt my fear.

39

I forgot that there might be
Fullness to replace fear
A consciousness of elegance
To replace eroded self-esteem,
Delight to replace Death.

Faith is a pivotal biblical concept; fear, a frequent visitor to biblical characters. Many times the texts tell us more about what we ought not do, as opposed to what we should do. Biblical faith varies from that of Abrahamic, encouraging faith to that of a Pauline, shipwrecked, and weakening faith experience. In the Hebrew Bible, the key meaning of faith is certainty or firmness; an experience of support of parent for child; to be certain about or be assured. This sense of assurance stands in contrast to our modern notion of our hopeful belief in something as possible.[1] This faith concerns human reaction to God's primary action. Theologically, faith relates to the individual and collective experience of vital, powerful relationships, embracing the whole of one's life amid new life and commitment. Faith involves the fear or respect of God over against a trust in God. In the New Testament, faith pertains to trust, to believing, to relying on; entrusting oneself in God. In Christian usage, faith means to believe, to obey, to trust, to hope, and as faithfulness.[2]

For the believer, faith awakens an awareness of the divine, and faith is awakened through hearing the preached word (Acts 3:16; Rom. 10:17). Such faith infuses one with confidence and boldness in Christ (Eph. 3:12), to confess (Rom. 10:8-9) and embody or be full of this faith (Acts 6:5). Faith cures us, makes us well (Mark 10:52), is healing and life-giving (Heb. 10:38), is ordained (Acts 6:7), and provides us the means by which we can be obedient (Heb. 11:8). For humanity, faith is not always active, embodied, and exemplary (1 Tim. 4:12). Sometimes human beings experience cowardly faith (Matt. 8:26), denial (1 Tim. 5:8), and emptiness (1 Cor. 15:17). Sometimes a weary and worn believer experiences an absence of faith (Heb. 4:2) where one is weak (Rom. 4:19) and void of faith (1 Cor. 15:14). Such a dearth of certainty and belief often emerges when we wear the cloaks of doubt, frailty, sickness, or fear.

Fear is just fear, neither good nor evil. The fear that stops us from crossing the street in front of a semitruck has a good result. The fear that stops us from being the loving creature God created us to be has a bad outcome. Denying that fear exists, however, compounds the situation. If we think of fear as a challenge of reconfiguring our energy, we will have many more possibilities. Some of us experience *FEAR* as *Fatal Exaggerated Agitated Reactions*. We react out of traumatized guilt, longing, low self-esteem, ignorance, and uncertainty. Feeding our bodies, minds, and spirits with such dread and trauma on a daily basis may push us into adrenaline overload, which can lower our immune system and set us up for many illnesses that would have been repelled otherwise. We can, however, view *FEAR* as *Facing Every Activity Regally*.

Such a transformed way of viewing fear is to experience the conversion of a troubling energy to a healthy passion. By facing every activity with a regal or noble spirit we commit ourselves, particularly in a religious sense, to putting our best foot forward in a majestic, admirable manner. Such movement illumines the light within us. In some instances the most noble action is a quiet, silent, and grace-filled waiting. In other circumstances the noblest action is prayerful, discerning, and faith-based steps. Whatever action we choose, we do so in concert with God's amazing grace. Such *GRACE* is *Godly Renewal: Activated, Certainly, and Eternally*. Such ongoing divine activity on behalf of humanity will sustain us and keep us when we are open to the presence of such power in our lives.

Meditation 4

Fear becomes my companion,
When weary eyes no longer see
The God within you,
The God within me,
Moving, troubling waters.

Then we might know
And believe and give thanks
Where we stand

41

Knowing that place,
Which is whole and complete:
the Abyss, the abode of nothingness.

Fear raps at my door,
The entrance to my heart,
Locks of hate and greed and self-loathing:
Do not keep the demonic at bay.

Fear is electric:
Charging the ions of my being.
Connectors too grounded in the baseness of now,
Drowning amid the vicissitudes,
Stunned by shallow promises
Of those unfamiliar with Grace and Faith.

Fear is a friend,
Among the possibilities
Of 8,640 seconds per day
In the Moment of Now,
This Instance of Joy
Created in the I-amness of God.

Fear, like static electricity, is annoying. Much of the garbage we attract in life clings by an attracted static and does not represent the whole picture. Sometimes we fear success; sometimes we fear failure. Frequently, we fear the unknown. Each day that we live is one of life and death: an invitation to newness, a eulogy for that which exists no more. Life, a complexity of dreams, realities, and mystery, depends on the sustaining properties of water. We need not fear water, but must also not build on the water's edge or riverfront if we are not prepared to greet a flood someday. The nature of rivers involves movement and overflowing. Grace, like water, flows and overflows. Grace, spiritual rain from the Divine, from the heavens, here on earth now, insures that fear need not overwhelm us because the reality of grace means we have options and choices. To stare fear in the face is to acknowledge that those moments of uncertainty, of thunderous rains and flooding, are soon transformed by the grace of certainty, silence, and new life. Only when we face fear head-on can we then move on.

To move on is not to run away. We cannot move from what we have not fully experienced. To face fear is to know fear on a visceral, physical, mental, emotional level. The way individuals experience fear involves their history, culture, personal habits, level of maturity, and level of consciousness. Critical to attaining intimacy with fear and then moving on is one's ability to stand amid both discomfort and the safety net of family, community, and self. Woven by grace, such a safety zone embodies spiritual gifts, particularly love and prophetic witness. Although prophets are usually not welcomed at home, we need those voices of wisdom and warning to face fear and to move on. Facing reality and discomfort takes courage, but such is not impossible and not always painful. In moments of awakening from the malaise of dreadful fear, one has a better sense of who she or he is, and is able to find purpose in life. To move on after facing the fear is to live. Ultimately, health and wholeness require being in the storm on the ship until the troubled waters and the rough rains are quiet. Healthy movement and change are major components for attaining and living liberative salvation.

To be free, liberated, or saved infers a grace-filled mode of being and existence in the world. Such salvation understands eschatology, an awareness and consciousness of being free now, which stands in tension with what is yet to come. To experience salvation is to know fear, without being a victim of fear. To be free of fear is not to be reckless, but sure in the love of God. To be free of fear is to accept the challenge of life as a ministry one is called to fulfill.

Seeing life as a ministry is the freedom assented to by those slave bards who sang, "And before I'll be a slave, I'll be buried in my grave, And go home to my Lord and be free."[3] To be free is to be open to possibilities, change, and responsibility for ourselves, our communities, and our ecology. True freedom is the ability to share a sense of liberation with others. True freedom can only be realized when one experiences a sense of salvation in the spiritual, physical, mental, emotional, communal, and economic facets of daily life. A faithful life of freedom does not negate the reality of fear, but does provide the tools and means for transcending the fear and making a difference.

Responsive Readings

Responsive Reading 1

Leader: Bless the God of life and love, who holds us when fear seeks to strangle us.

People: **Hallelujah! The victory is in the blessedness of God: our Shepherd, our Mother, our Redeemer, and our Friend.**

Leader: All praises to the One who gives life and love, compassion and hope, empowering us to spread a gospel of faith and renewal.

People: **In thanksgiving we come to give honor and glory to God and to the children of God. We pledge to see the image of God in every human creature, that we might celebrate a community of faithful witnesses.**

Leader: Exalted is the God who gives hope and certainty; the One who calls us to serve, and who liberates and loves us into wellness and solidarity.

People: **Great is the Spirit that comforts and empowers. Great is the Spirit that helps us face fear as an opportunity to be people of faith.**

Leader: Because God is God, we give witness to that which may appear to be impossible possibilities to us, but are possible realities to God.

All: **In celebration of God and life, we give thanks. In honor of difficult times, in praise of joy, renewal, and love, we give thanks. For the gift of facing fear and moving on, we bless God's awesome love and care.**

As Ecclesiastes people, we realize that there is a time and a place for everything under the sun. We recognize that life has its own vitality and that the days of our lives are filled with possibilities in what often feels like uncertainty. In the Wisdom literature of the Hebrew Bible, the writers make it clear that God is behind life and thus life is in order, even if it seems to be chaotic. Many times in dealing with fear we forget to praise. We forget these are moments to draw closer to God. Sometimes we are so trapped by what we "used to do" and what "could have" or "should have" been that we cannot exist in the exquisite "moment of now." Sometimes today is the tomorrow that we dreaded yesterday. When we exist in the now, in the present, we have the possibility of living life at a more conscious level.

Such a level of consciousness reminds us that as we praise, we have opportunities to embrace *FAITH,* as *F*ervent *A*nticipatory *I*ncarnated *T*otal *H*ealing. Such faith is the realized passion of an individual for intimacy with God. As we anticipate and actively wait to experience the Divine, we celebrate the incarnated, embodied love of God within us that connects with the Divine and with one another. Such realizations move us toward a place where old wounds can be healed. The ongoing process of healing makes us more alive each day. This level of consciousness anesthetizes us from looking the other way and feigning ignorance when there is a need for societal transformation.

Responsive Reading 2

Leader: Fear, in the respect and honor of God, is the beginning of Wisdom, the beginning of an appreciation of God's greatness and loving power.

People: **We honor God and our neighbors as we all commune in love—growing, not yielding, to the fear and ignorance often created by difference and doubt.**

Leader: We embrace fear as an opportunity to grow closer to God and to one another. Fear becomes a catalyst for change as we discern the path of righteousness, justice, mercy, and love.

People: **With God as our helper and strength, we affirm our faith and hope. We believe in the healing power of love and in the certainty that God will never leave us or forsake us.**

Leader: We lift our eyes to Mt. Zion and await God's revelation as we wait, listen, love, share, hope, and work to build a togetherness that brings joy and fits us to face all difficulties, all pain.

People: **Created in God's image, we look for the best in others and in ourselves. We stand together amid our differences, grounded in our ancestral faith, of those who have gone before.**

Leader: Recognizing the joys and sorrows of history, we learn from our past, affirm our present reality, and look to daily moments of joy, hope, and wholeness, to the glory of God.

All: **We wait for God and hold forth in courage, that fear might caution but not overwhelm us as we lean on God's everlasting arms.**

When fraught with fear, despair, and hopelessness we are reminded to have the faith at least the size of the mustard seed. Our faith may not always be strong, but we are called to be ever vigilant and prayerful. The increase in fear often means the decrease in our faith. Pretending fear is not present is not realistic, nor is it realistic to think we can live life to the fullest without a visit from fear. By embracing fear we learn that the fear is not bigger than we are or stronger than our faith. When we experience our faith as a gift from God and are closely connected to God, we are enfolded in a life preserver of grace. Threads of grace surround us for our Creator cares for us deeply. We experience God's revelatory nature in who we are and in the glorious riches of nature that surround us.

How blessed we are to be in faithful relationship with One so loving, so artistic, so caring. How meaningful to appreciate the majesty of creation and see our own nobility and dignity as part of God's beauty.

Responsive Reading 3

Leader: Great is the faithfulness of God and of God's people, who are not shackled by the fears of doubt, hate, anger, fear, and prejudice.

People: **In faith we stand before God and ask for blessings of clear thinking, honest living, and a spirit of generosity.**

Leader: We celebrate the reality and good news of God's amazing, awesome love. This faith commemorates that God's love and our desire for God's covenant relationship is life-giving and complete.

People: **By faith we live, dream, work, and see. By faith we gain communal strength as we celebrate our differences.**

Leader: By faith we live with the tensions between the known and the unknown, with courage and fear, and with hope and desperation.

People: **We rejoice and give thanks for the opportunity to live a life of gratitude as witness to those who are still searching for divine intimacy.**

Leader: We thank God for renewing our empty, dying faith with an ever-strengthening, sustaining love. As adopted children of faith, we celebrate all unique life and invite divine wisdom in all we say and do.

All: **Just as God spoke all creation into being, we speak together today. We acknowledge God's rule over us and we stand as many, as one. We depend on God; may others depend on us.**

The dynamics and realm of faithfulness cannot be measured. God's faithfulness gives us abundant life, protection, and saving love. Because of God's faithfulness others can hear and experience our faith in action. Because of our faith we believe, and we live a righteous life realized in our thoughts and our deeds. The gift of faith moves us to be faithful stewards of ourselves and our resources. We rejoice not for self-aggrandizement, but we rejoice because our faith makes us whole, giving, and loving people. Our faith helps cure our physical, emotional, mental, spiritual, and economic needs. Faith allows us to have a new perspective and the courage to engage the support of others. Faith serves as a catalyst for our creativity. When we can imagine, we can develop new ways of doing old things. Faith accords us spiritual powers, wisdom, and vision whereby we honor God's creation.

Responsive Reading 4

Leader: The beauty of God and the beauty of the earth signify a redeeming faithfulness, hope, and joy, which floods our souls with anticipation.

People: **We come with a thirst for God only quenched by grace and possibility. We rejoice in the faith of Sarah and Hagar, in the wilderness of their lives.**

Leader: We offer thanks for the moments of wilderness and oasis, grounded in our common faith, deepening our commitment to the union we know with our God.

People: **Blessedness and joy are ours as the household of faith. Faith fuels our ministries and sustains our quest for wholeness and community.**

Leader: Faith nurtures our spiritual, moral, mental, and emotional well-being. With faith we live through the storms and valleys, amid victory and death.

People: **We gather today asking God's blessings and praising God for all that we have received by grace. This grace gives us life and abundance.**

Leader: Praise God from whom all blessings pour out afresh among us; for the gifts of faith and its abiding hope and love. Renew us and make our little faith great.

All: **We submit that our faith is fashioned as the foundation of our lives, making us righteous, willing to be God's people and to be with God's people everywhere.**

Often we think of beauty in the limited terms of external, physical beauty. We forget about the many ways beauty exists in God's world. So focused, we miss out on the beauty of nature, time, and the way in which the human body is a superb machine—the architecture of it is beauty in itself. Faith is also beautiful as it is pleasing in bringing solace and comfort. The possibilities of a life grounded in ever-increasing faith are beautiful as we have greater sensual perception of our surroundings. Faith is beautiful in its elegance: so powerful and delicate, so full when present. Such faith is our foundation for life and spirituality, and molds our relationship with God. Faith conquering fear provides the energy to make one more step, to pass through drudgery yet fully experience it. Faith helps us stand at times of doubt and endure until our confidence returns. Faith is such a part of our reality that we sometimes take it for granted. We must always be mindful that faith is a gift of God for the people of God called to do good in the world.

Prayers of Commitment

Prayer of Commitment 1

As children of God we rejoice and are exceedingly glad for the possibilities and new experiences that we will know as we are daily empowered to overcome the paralyzing nature of fear. We embrace fear as a time of growth, knowing we go not to the depths of despair, but to the valleys of change and the mountaintops of growth. May the words of our mouths be utterances of faith, seeking understanding in ways that enhance our community and ourselves.

Grant us, O Creator, the wisdom to make sound decisions, to be good neighbors, to be more like You each day. We offer thanks for Your words of hope and all the beauty of the earth that surrounds us. We commit to facing fear and moving on in ways that glorify You, Gracious Spirit. Renew us as we share our faith and minister to those yet trapped by fear.

Words of prayer comfort, console, and commend. Our words of faith bring solace and cheer, empathy and an understanding spirit. In offering prayer about embracing our fear we indicate that we will show up for the wonderful moments and difficult times. In praying about fear we give others the courage to face their own inadequacies, doubts, and confusions.

Offering thanks demonstrates our allegiance to the Author of our faith. Renewal provides an ongoing sense of growth, stability, and the room to examine life's issues from varying perspectives. Prayer about fear heightens our own awareness about the depths of such an experience without giving up in despair or futility. The act of praying about fear robs fear of its power to suppress.

Prayer of Commitment 2

In the dew of morning, in the brightness of noon, and in the quiet of night, we praise God. We invite a spirit of contentment, hope, and renewal at this strategic point in the lives of our community. We receive God's gift of faith. May this faith provide the assurance that we can sustain our daily walk with You.

As we experience Your revelation in our daily lives we promise to see the beauty of the earth and of one another. We want to be faithful stewards of all that You have given us. We welcome the gift to bear witness of our faith to others.

Understanding that righteousness is the work of the Spirit through faith, we receive Your blessing of mending our hearts. We confess our doubt and disbelief. We celebrate our resurrection from mistrust and fear to renewed confidence in the power of Your love, mercy, and justice.

In quiet gratitude and loud hope, we thank You.

Overcoming fear with faith is a daily adjustment. Such fine-tuning of our life's strategies and energies mean that we are able to live life more fully and know a sense of fulfillment that we might otherwise lack. Such faith-based awareness allows individuals and communities "variations on the themes of life." A faith-based life invigorates our commitment to stewardship and lessens our experience of the mundane. Renewing faith forges our dialogues with the Divine and with others toward more inclusivity and wealth. The results of a prayerful life provides fertile incentive to those who may be seeking the good news of the gospel.

Prayer of Commitment 3

As faith energizes us to embrace love and live in community, we rejoice that this day is the Day of God, where we need know no fear, frustration, and deceit. You are our lily of the valley, our bright and shining star, and our rock in a weary land.

In darkness or light, in sorrow or in joy, we turn to You, Gracious Spirit, for you are life. Your gift of faith allows us to count our life as gift and joy. In response to Your faith, we affirm our willingness to be your light to those who are yet in darkness.

In thanksgiving we offer our lives to be lived by Your pleasure, honoring Your call on our lives, walking by faith. Daily we commit to spending time to listen for Your voice. We pledge that You are the potter and we are the clay, willing and ready to be molded to Your faithful service of love.

Children have an unspoiled faith that their parents will care for them and provide for all their needs. Infants make a joyful noise to this effect through their tears and crying. As people of God, we also have a faith that God, as our parent, cares for us and will provide for our needs. In response, we make a joyful noise in songs, prayers, sermons, and other liturgical acts. Joyful noises with joyful voices are juxtaposed to the aches and pains of life. Psalm 150 tells us where, why, and how to praise God: in the sanctuary, for God's mighty works, with trumpet, lute, harp, tambourines, flute, strings, cymbals, dancing, and with everything that has breath. With praise, we say *yes*. With praise, we give thanks. With praise, we teach others to live, to believe, to give.

Prayer of Commitment 4

We come with thankful hearts during these times of growth and high expectations. We proclaim Your generosity in every area of our lives. We offer our lives as faithful, liturgical reminders of Your benevolence.

May our faith be so unusual that new believers look not to us, but to the source of this trust. We celebrate Your awesome wonder, encouraged by Your commitment to us. As Your grace alone saves us, we falter not at the law or the cross, but focus on the lived reality of your love.

May we begin to see the image of God in ourselves and in those around us. May our hearts beat to the pulse of divine love and joy. May we stand in faith, not in judgment, as we witness your mysterious, indescribable love in the little things we do for others. Grant us a peaceful, serene presence as we grow in Your grace.

Most of what we learn, we learn through imitation. We see and hear others, and in turn, we repeat what other individuals say or do. We are not only called to imitate God in faithfulness, but to teach others to do likewise. Imitation is one of the highest forms of adulation and praise. By imitating the faith of God, we praise God. Faith provides some of the strategy for living a life where peace passes all understanding. Faith gives us the incentive to live life another day. In faith our work and our lives speak for us—and speak for us well.

---

1. R. Laird Harris, ed., *Theological Wordbook of the Old Testament*, vol. 1 (Chicago: Moody Press, 1980), 51.

2. Gerhard Kittle, ed., *Theological Dictionary of the New Testament*, vol. 6 (Grand Rapids: Eerdmans, 1969), 174-215.

3. See the traditional African American spiritual "Oh, Freedom."

Chapter 3

Faith: Covenant Relationships in Action

An eloquence,
Of joining the many and the few,
The saved, the lost, and
The not-so-saved.

Perpetual angst and misery,
Slay sweet peace and place
Of divine stability.
Conjoined eternal crossroads
Of immediacy and distance.

God chooses us each day.
Some days we choose God,
Other times, we pretend that
God does not exist:
A rupture that displaces and jolts us
Toward apathy or reformation.

Covenant invites:
Honest talk, plain dealing,
Praise, cross-examination,
Clarifying real
Times of possibility when
There is nowhere else to go.

*F*aith moves us to active covenantal being and existence. The biblical notion of convenant involves a powerful declaration of intimacy, faith, and relatedness. A covenant in a theological engagement between the Divine and humanity involves promises and commitment on the part of both parties. In the Hebrew Bible, covenant is a grace-filled binding agreement, as God declares, "I will be your God and you will be my people," in love. In the New Testament, one key experience of covenant is the revelation or disclosure of God's will. Covenantal faith involves a concept, a process, and a community. Such faith involves the experience of desire and of wanting to be in loving relationship. Collectively, a community embraces a vigorous faith, empowered by the Holy Spirit, to live, work, teach, and learn together. This kind of faith prepares individual and collective hearts to be transformed. Sometimes the mysteries of life seem so overarching that reality does not make sense. These nonsensical moments are the very times when one must hold on to active faith.

Meditations

Meditation 1

The faithfulness alive in us
Mirrors ancient hopeful belief,
Personified in
The God who sees and knows,
The I-amness of the God who loves and destroys,
The courage and cowardice of Abraham,
The fancy and fear of Sarah,
The victimage and victory of Hagar.

The destitution and dream-vision of Joseph,
The obstinence and obedience of Moses,
The enthusiasm and extraneousness of Zipporah,
The pity and prayerful drunkness of Hannah,
The stupidity and strength of Samson,
The seductiveness and gentleness of Ruth:
These forge our spiritual DNA.

We move in the world
Amid contemplation and contemptuousness,
Joy and injustice,
Wondering
Do we really believe?

We need the faith of our communities to nurture, sustain, and sometimes shield us from ourselves when we live at the gates of fear, emptiness, and loneliness. Often faith may be as elusive as the clouds. We see clouds and we know they bring rain. We can fly through, above, or under clouds, but we cannot capture or contain them. Clouds are light, filmy, visible masses of water particles or ice that appear as fog, mist, or haze, usually suspended far above us in the sky like the paradox of our faith experience. Sometimes we take comfort in knowing that the fog is there. Other times, the fog clouds our view.

We hold so to our faith that we may not see what lies before us, where God may be taking us to new vistas, new mysteries, and new ministries. One of the places where the children of Israel often experienced God was in the pillar of cloud of the Lord, which guided them by day, and the pillar of fire of the Lord, which provided them with light to travel by night (Exod. 13:21; 14:24; Num. 9:16; 9:21). Sometimes the glory or the voice of God appears as a cloud or within a cloud, in the temple or up in high mountains (Ezek. 10:4; Matt. 17:5; Mark 9:7; Luke 9:35). Such visible manifestations of God, or theophanies, appear throughout the Bible. The irony of clouds, as they mask and reveal, is the paradox of our faith experience. Such faith experiences undergird the experience of the biblical covenants between God and humanity.

Covenant intimacy is God's gracious guarantee to provide for us. In Genesis 6:18, God makes a covenant with Noah that all else will be destroyed save Noah and those he takes in the ark. Further, God makes a covenant with Noah and his descendants to never again destroy creation by water and establishes the sign of this everlasting covenant: a rainbow (Gen. 9:8-17). In Genesis 12, 15, and 17, God covenants with Abraham and with the whole human race: gifts of land, gifts of being fruitful in perpetuity, and the gift of being our God.

In Genesis 17, God changes the name of Abram, meaning *high father*, to Abraham, *father of a multitude*. God also changes the name of Abraham's wife, Sarai, meaning *mockery*, to Sarah, *princess*. These name changes of the key players in this biblical saga mark a change in the relationship. God reaffirms divine commitment to the house of Abraham and Abraham's descendants for all generations to come. The giving of the blessing of covenant and the openness to receiving the blessing of covenant is faith in action: an affirmation and living out of belief, commitment, assurance, trust, and allegiance. This trust, commitment, and assurance undergirds the experience of the covenantal ethos of Psalm 23. When we rest, God restores our soul. God brings back our health and beauty, the same beauty and wholeness that we had at our birth. God returns and restores our *nephesh*, our vitality, and the essence of us as breathing creatures.

In the prologue to John's Gospel, John proclaims that we all receive grace upon grace. That is, Moses gave the law, but grace and truth come through Christ Jesus. That overflowing grace brings revelation and salvation. God, the *Logos*, is with us. In the last chapter of the Revelation of John, the author reports that God lives with us, God is our God, and God will wipe all tears from our eyes. With this gracious gift of God we become true community and true friends, as believers in a covenantal relationship with God and with one another. Covenant friendship, as faith in action, transcends the superficial to unite the heart and soul in testimony to the resurrection of Jesus Christ. We all become one body in God, and in God we become holy. In choosing to take Jesus as our friend, we open our door to holiness, to community, and to genuine friendship.

Meditation 2

God, faithful, everlasting,
Calls to humanity to love,
A passion for life,
Honored by intimacy,
Profound in our own createdness.

Faith speaks loudly,
Above the cacophony of pain,
Lived by many oppressed,
Labeled as Other
By those who think
They're really in charge,
Whose power lasts for but an instant.

Time, the gift of now,
Brings renewal for building faith,

Despite the contradictions,
Which appear to be devastating,
But may only be illusion.

The stories of biblical and contemporary lives bespeak a
faithful God, a merciful, loving being who created us to be in
relationship with us. The lives of Enoch, Noah, Jacob, Joseph,
Moses, Hannah, Deborah, and countless others reveal a life of
convenant faith that shaped their actions and the way they
existed in the world. In the lives of early church fathers such as
Tertullian, Augustine, and Origen, and in the experiences of
medieval mystics such as Hildegard von Bingen and Teresa of
Avila, in the lives of the Reformers such as Luther, Calvin, and
Hus, faith was part of their viscera, their pilgrimage, their
thinking, and their beliefs. In the lives of Søren Kierkegaard,
Karl Barth, the Niebuhrs, Hans Küng, Martin Luther King, Jr.,
Malcolm X, Howard Thurman, Mother Seton, Rosa Parks,
Sister Thea Bowman, Mother Teresa, Dorothy Day, and count-
less other saints, visionaries, and leaders, faith has been their
ground of being.

Love is powerful. Love helps us transcend, grow, and actu-
alize fully the capacity of what it means to be human and to be
in community in the world. This movement is sometimes
fraught with resistance from those who want things to remain
the same. Other times this covenantal love is a move to joyful
action, made visible in thousands of random acts of kindness
done by thousands of people each day, not for the sake of
national or international acclaim, but because people care. So
often we hear phrases of doom and gloom about the current
status of the world. The actions of God and humanity taken in
toto rebuke that assumption.

There were "no good old days." When we note the devasta-
tion of bubonic plague from the thirteenth to seventeenth centuries, the deaths because of polluted water, and communicable
diseases and viruses prior to immunizations and antibiotics, we
see there were no good old days. The hundreds of lynchings,
the selling of women for dowries in marriage, and the many
people who have died in construction and westward migration
signifies that there were no good old days. Japanese intern-

ment camps and the Trail of Tears, our history of slavery, Jim Crow, and segregation indicates that there were no good old days. When we think of children who have had no childhood, we know there were no good old days. Only when we see faith in action, when we can appreciate the glorious artistic, musical, and literary works throughout time, do we realize that God has sustained us throughout history—past, present, future—the essence of good days. In that celebration of goodness we realize the profound gift of our own createdness.

Out of our desperation, insecurity, fear, and ignorance, we often separate others and then target them for oppression, as we need to feel righteous and superior. We often think we are in charge and that the sun rises and sets on our own idiosyncrasies. We must hold in tension the scriptures of the centrality and the miniscule role of humanity to the whole order of creation. Given that God cares about the lilies of the field, who do not work but are resplendent, surely God cares for every component of human life (Matt. 7:28-34; Luke 12:27-31). Conversely, God asks Job where Job was when God created the foundation of the world, indicating that Job's situation is only one experience that pales in comparison (Job 38). Much in our lives is this mystery and paradox. Much is glorious and becomes even more so when lived from a context of faithful action. Amid paradox, mystery, and change, the relationship between God and humanity becomes more amazing and awesome. In celebrating this gift of grace and the gift of faith, we are moved toward redemption, renewal, and reformation. The experience of change embodied in being redeemed, renewed, reformed, and saved is to encounter lived faith. If we focus only on the pain and contradictions, our view of reality becomes an illusion—a mirage, a fantasy, a deception. For as long as the eternal God keeps a covenant faith for us, we know hope, possibility, and renewal: the tenets of the gospel message that God is with us.

Meditation 3

Faith, the context for healing,
Becomes a catalyst for well-being
Amid the divine gaze,
Remaking dry bones,

Reshaping paralyzed limbs,
Restoring ill health.

Faith: a process, a power, a presence of God,
Energizes our tired minds,
Regulates our hearts,
Renews our tired bodies,
Excites our broken spirits,
Makes us whole.

Faith serves as a divine lens,
Showing us the density of pain;
Helping us to rebel to that which needs to change:
Shielding us from hopelessness,
Reminding us of the sacredness,
Which made, sustains, and keeps us.

In the quiet of midnight or the bustle of noonday, God is with us. Many messages bombard our presence in the many moments, the sixty seconds per minute, 3,600 seconds per hour, 86,400 seconds per day, 2,592,000 per month, and approximately 31,104,000 seconds per year. In the majesty of these moments faith brings about healing. God's faith is that power that can bring about miracles. And miracles occur every day: our bodies function magnificently, babies are born healthy, surgeons perform life-saving procedures, composers write music, visual artists fashion beauty fixed in various mediums, dancers and gymnasts shape their bodies in intricate ways, and we fly in outer space. In these and other ways God endows us with magnificence and miracles of healing and health. Sometimes, despite all we do, healing as restored health does not occur. The possibility for healing occurs in our lives because of the faithful covenant between God and humanity. Thus faith is not only a context, but is vitality. Such vitality is a process, a power of God's presence with us. Faith is a divine gift, and the giver accompanies the gift to make the experience holy. Holiness makes our lives and ourselves sacred. The realization of being made sacred in any of those daily 86,400 seconds is incarnated love realized.

Love in action is more powerful than prophecy, symphonic

sounds, and sacrifice. First Corinthians 13 extols the power and promise of love, the love that is a catalyst for faith. Love stands above envy and boastfulness. Love is patient, kind, polite, and embraces community. Love transcends retribution, limits, and conceit. Love is everlasting, mature, and a gift of the spirit. Loving faith provides the oasis in the desert, the place of refreshment and regeneration. For many, such an experience of loving faith is a *kairos* moment—a resurrection, a rebirth, a revival. Revival is a time where individuals and communities can resuscitate, rejuvenate, revitalize. Sometimes hurt, trauma, and self-doubt can press our fragile selves to an abyss from where we feel we cannot return. These are the moments when our community, family, and/or network need to provide healthy life supports to sustain us through our crises. A critical component of this rejuvenation process is faith. With the strength, the prayer, and the care of a community that can be the living witness of faith in action, one can come to a sense of peace, to periods of revitalization, and to new places of experiencing self and God.

Often the place of the desert, of standing naked before God and ultimately encountering our true selves, is not only a place of the unknown, but a fearful place to be. Who is God for us? Does God really care about our individual and collective lives? God is love and God created humanity for the sake of relationship. God knows our story, our cares, and our fears. God's justice and mercy in context with God's love is the cushion of salvation ready to hold us when we stand ready to have a more intense Divine-human relationship. The desert is usually an arid, barren land, desolate and sparsely occupied, and is often a quiet place of life. In the Arizona desert there is a most incredible tract called the Joshua Tree Forest: tall-branched, arborescent yuccas with short leaves and clustered greenish-white flowers. Some have two or three main branches, others have as many as a dozen—such life in Arizona and southern California! Prior to driving through the Joshua Tree Forest there is no indication of what lies ahead. Yet one can die in the desert from exposure to tremendous heat during the day and cold at night. In order to experience faith in action as covenant, one must often die to old ways of being, thinking, and doing. Initially it may appear that one can only choose to rebel. Rebelling is several steps above lethargy and unconsciousness. In the process of rebelling, the desire for newness and wholeness may arise. In that moment, one goes to the desert to touch the sacredness of God, ourselves, and our neighbor as we come alive.

Meditation 4

Life, like rain,
Condensed atmospheric vapors,
Falls and makes all things wet,
Awaiting the sun for light,
Drying and warming,
Together bringing forth new realities.

Rain, with lightning and thunder,
Electrifying atmosphere, discharging,
The sudden expansion of charged air,
Nature's symphonic dance
We know and can't control.

Nature's symphonic dance
Illumines the incredibility of God,
The magnificence of creation,
The love-binding covenant,
The blessing of faithful action,
The sacredness of being you.

Water is a life-giving and death-causing element. We need water to survive. In too large a quantity with too great a force, in hurricanes, floods, and spring thaws, that same water kills. When we operate out of bondage to our anger and rage or when we shut down and freeze out life itself, our lives are like the floods or arctic ice. A piece of such ice triggered the demise of the allegedly invincible ship *Titanic*. Some of our lives are a lot like the *Titanic*. As we plunge ahead in the deep waters we fail to realize there are icebergs nearby; in moments of smooth sailing or distress we need the assurance and stability of covenant faith. Covenant faith provides a safety zone where we can hover until help comes, where we can live our daily lives, where babies are born, and where all of us can die.

61

Covenant faith is the assurance of grace that sustains us when we are open to that power.

Like the rain, life's events sometimes come in soft, gentle drops or thunderous, electrifying upheaval. In the midst of the gentle sprinkle we experience peace, become relaxed, and are often able to be at one with ourselves and created order. In the moments of torrential downpour we often experience a restlessness that changes to deep concern when our lives and property seem to be on the verge of destruction. In the winters of harsh weather and discontent or in the springs of re-creation and all things made new, we are challenged by the vicissitudes of life. These ebbs and flows in our existence often precede monumental changes symbolized by nature's symphonic dances—the many colors of creativity, numerous textures, qualities, and sounds from triple forte to incredibly soft. Thus there are many things in our lives that we cannot control, but we can have a healthy outlook when we ground our realities in faithful, covenantal action.

Such action is prayerful and participatory. In the context of God's great, enduring, extensive, and reliable faith (Lam. 3:23; Ps. 100:5; Ps. 36:5), humanity knows assurance, a certainty of divine care. This covenantal, foundational faith illumines the incredibility of God, the potentiality of God's children, and the household of faith to work for the good of all (Gal. 6: 10). Such faith does not measure itself in superficial ways, self-aggrandizement, or the acclaim of others. This faith in action is in action simply because God freely gives the gift of faith, and humanity can freely choose to operate out of such divine benevolence. With the lens of covenant faith, one can see through murky waters and stained-glass windows. Faithful vision has a way of letting one transcend the mundane to view the magnificent, interfacing into soliloquies and choruses of thanksgiving that inspire us to act—becoming sacred, becoming whole, becoming you.

Responsive Readings

Responsive Reading 1:

Leader: Praise Great Spirit of faithful love and promise, give us Your mercy. Renew our hearts to an openness to receive You, as You reshape us.

People: **You are loving-kindness and mercy; Your grace is sufficient and life-giving. Blessed be Your name as we express Your covenant love.**

Leader: Your faithfulness lives from everlasting to everlasting and Your freedom is never ending. Open our eyes that we may fully see You.

People: **Deliver us from those times when we forget to honor You. Remind us always of Your gracious presence and help us be Your representatives.**

Leader: Just as Abraham honored Your covenant, we lift our voices in celebration of Your tremendous love and commitment to You.

People: **Your faith calls us to be in intimate relationship, to honor Your essence within us, daily worshiping and adoring You out of joy.**

Leader: Your generosity is more intense than the bluest sky, is warmer than the hottest flame, is more beautiful than the most radiant sky.

All: **Holy, holy, holy, You are Creator. We rejoice and give thanks that Your covenant with us is ever new and everlasting.**

We are called to praise God in God's holy place in the heavens, because of the divine mighty words and because of divine greatness. We are called to praise God with trumpet, lute and harp, tambourines and dancing, flute and strings and cymbals. Everything that breathes is called to praise God. Psalms, a book of hymns, poems, and prayers, begin with moral teachings about human life and end in praise. Praise is the celebration of God: the acts of adoration and the acts of homage. When connected to faithful covenant action, one praises God daily. There is a release and a joy unspeakable when one engages in praise, particularly praise with power from the Holy Spirit. Praise is effortless, as we are children of God called to a committed relationship with God, ourselves, and our neighbor. Praise is an extension of those relationships. In praise, the relationship becomes illuminated so that when the scales of death, distrust, and denial fall from our eyes we can then see not only the power of God, but also the illumination of God, reflected back in our lives. Such grace is the incarnated generosity that ever sustains our faith. To honor an everlasting covenant is to be in and with God. To be ultimately intimate with God is to know a state beyond compare, a divine ecstasy, a delight, a rapture, a blessedness, and a soulful tune signifying greatness.

Responsive Reading 2

Leader: In covenant, obedient trust we look to You, Gracious God, for love and guidance, power and joy, because You have made us wonderfully.

People: **In covenant faith help our unbelief, quiet our doubt, and help us confront our guilt, that we may love You and ourselves more justly.**

Leader: We know the complexity of Your faith transcends our ability to understand. Yet in Your mercy you come to us, inviting us daily to be in faithful covenant relationship.

People: **As we listen for Your revelation help us discern, know, accept, and be committed to Your disclosure of Your grace.**

Leader: Help us see the holiness and grace of Your faithful covenantal reality in history. Help us respond in faith as individuals and community.

People: **Help us be so inspired and in unity with Christ that You will compel us to live out a faithful life as celebration of You and as witness to others.**

Leader: In the mystery and certainty of the ways and means of faith we come before You on our pilgrimage to become more grace-filled.

All: **Great is God; greatly to be praised. In promise, we humble ourselves as recipients of Your generous faith that sustains and blesses us for all time.**

To be confident is to be certain, to have full assurance of mind, or to have a firm belief in the reality or trustworthiness of another. Such confidence inspires a boldness and a courage to persevere that overcomes suspicion or distrust. Confidence in God gives us a marvelous sense of power and joy, which gives us a hopeful, generous way of being in the world. We have a sense of a benevolent God who has created a vast abundance, that humanity might take pleasure in this fullness and be good stewards over such blessings as our context becomes generosity. In times of social action our mind-set embraces a surety that God is on our side—on the side of those who believe, who care, and who love. God takes delight and pleasure in our healing, our conversions, our health, and our salvation. As God's faith generates our faith and our faithfulness, in times of quiet we may often hear God's still, small voice that says, "Here I am, the I-am, who is always becoming, who is here on your behalf, Beloveds."

The I-amness, the presence of God, can temper our unbelief, soothe our doubts, and calm our fears. The I-amness of God is so amazing that God has the room for us to come as we are, to do the best we can, to help deal with our various identity crises, until our own I-amness mirrors the I-amness of God. Such is the gift of consummate love. The fertile nature of the beingness of God is so mysterious, yet so creative and so available to us if we but ask and seek. In the process, God's reality does not oppress but heightens our own. The beingness and existence of God serves as a foundation for a faithful covenant and for God's beingness within us. We can be comforted by the historical record of mystics and other holy persons. There two biblical accounts of holy persons being present and then disappearing into the heavens: when Elijah rides the chariot into the heavens (2 Sam. 2), and in the Transfiguration of Jesus (Mark 9) when Elijah and Moses appear. In the Transfiguration account Jesus remained while Elijah and Moses, who had died centuries before, appeared and then disappeared. In the case of

Elijah, it was his time to die. Thus we need not fear the power and love of God embodied in covenant faith and action.

Responsive Reading 3

Leader: Covenant faith is a confessing confidence that gives us the strength to speak with our mouths and our hearts of God's goodness, glory, and love.

People: **Confessing faith is a way of life centered on the purpose and meaning of God. In our lives, hopes, and experiences we have a chance to make our God-given, sustaining covenant faith visible.**

Leader: In the daily rhythm of our lives our gifts of faith bring about healing and newness, even saying to the mountain, "Be moved."

People: **Even when we experience cowardly and hesitant faith we can hold fast to the faith of our ancestors, our community, and our loved ones.**

Leader: We stand in doubt, yet we are comforted by a divine covenant faith, which reminds us that weeping and tears linger at midnight, but joy comes in the morning.

People: **In the morning of our lives we awaken to a new day, new hopes, and new outlooks for living this twenty-four hours amid God's faithful covenant, the source of our strength, hope, and consolation.**

Leader: Each day is a new day, a day fashioned by God; moments of holiness and of love if we but trust and remain open to faithful covenantal grace.

All: **Glory and honor! Thank You, gracious God, for the gifts of faith, love, and life. Fix our inmost selves that we may embrace Your covenant faith.**

Confessing faith is proclamation in action. In the making-known of one's faith to another, one is able to move from self-reflection and personal piety to community engagement and liturgy. To verbalize one's faith to another is an act of worship and witness. The speaking is the telling of the story, an affirmation and recitation of the activity of God in one's life, which also becomes an invitation to others to experience the goodness, glory, and love of God. The confession allows a kind of intimacy that can be vital to the total health and well-being. Such intimacy is foundational to becoming aware of God and God's purpose and meaning for our lives. In this God-given faith made visible, we build community and sustain one another. As our gifts of faith bring about healing and newness we hold fast to the faith of our ancestors. This great heritage of trust and belief helps sustain us and fortify us, to see the image of God in one another. In our joys and sorrows, in our highs and lows, on the mountaintops and in the valleys, faithful covenant honors and protects us. In these relationships God provides bounteously and lovingly. Even in moments of mystery or angst, covenant faith maintains us.

Responsive Reading 4

Leader: Faith in the fullness of each moment embraces mystery and mischievousness as we approach each day with a childlike curiosity and innocence.

People: **We wear our covenant faith in innocence and desire as a loving garment prepared for us by God to equip us for love, witness, and solidarity.**

Leader: Covenant faith is our shelter amid green valleys and cloudy abysses that seem to be obstacles but which are really moments to discern again who God is calling us to be.

People: **By grace we claim the cloak of faith as we come alive in God. Our faith energizes us to renewal and a lightness of heart.**

Leader: From the ecstasy and joy of birth to the finality and consolation of death, we are never alone, for God never ever forsakes us.

People: **Hallelujah to the hope and joy of the faith that God awakens in us. God, the potter, remolds and fashions the clay of us as mighty vessels of loving, healthy faith.**

Leader: God fills these human vessels with blessed waters of hope, joy, and salvation. This witness, ordained by God, brings us into the company of the cloud of witnesses to God's amazing grace.

All: **Blessed be! Blessed be! We take delight in God's faithful call on our lives to fulfill our ministries, as lay and clergy, to study and equip ourselves to be the light, the salt, the faithful neighbors to the world.**

Prayers of Commitment

Prayer of Commitment 1

In humility and gratitude, Gracious God, we recommit our lives, our all, to the faithful covenant between You and us. We confess our unbelief, our fears, and our uncertainty. Even in our blessedness we often fail to carry through on our promises. There are days when in practice we reject You and ourselves. There have been moments when we celebrated our faith by embodying our beliefs in comfort by praying for those who by Your grace experienced healing. For this we give thanks.

Many times our faith has been too small, cowardly, and weak. We have been so paralyzed by fear that we think everything else revolves around us. We think that all the issues are issues about us. There have been many times when we have lost perspective about what is important. We open our hearts, minds, and spirits to divine discernment.

We promise to engage in daily prayer, lifting our praise and concerns, and to engage in daily meditation, where we can open ourselves to hearing God's response to our queries.

In our faith journey our growth requires being clear about our strengths and weaknesses, our knowledge and ignorance, and our desires and fears. In learning about who we are and having the courage to name our spiritual assets and liabilities we can then begin to address the necessary changes for health and wholeness. During our moments of awareness and enlightenment we see who we are. We then remember whose we are and where we ought to be in our faith journey. Being in a covenant with God means to be in a living process. To be in denial about reality does not alter the facts, nor do we become healthier. To refuse to change for the good is often worse than death itself, as we then break the covenant, and hope dims for transformation and recovery. The willingness to be open to confession is the beginning of new life. When this openness forms the larger context for all our lives, we then move toward total liberation and salvation, which affects all we do in all relationships. This kind of marked change requires prayer and supportive community. Prayer must be a dialogue: a dialogue that is praise, disclosure, and request before and of God, followed by moments of quiet that one may hear, discern, and feed on divine response.

Prayer of Commitment 2

Gracious God, we read the texts of Abraham's faith, of Sarah's laughter, and of Hagar's seeing You. Sometimes these texts nourish and nurture us; other times these texts confuse us. Often when we pray we are afraid to listen for You, so we fail to hear Your response. Sometimes we break our covenants because it feels that maintaining this bond with You is too difficult. In those quiet moments we are unable to believe that You loved us so much that You became incarnated as Jesus, the Christ. Sometimes we do not live out this faith. We know that because of Your grace and love we have the option of living in abundant joy. Yet we often live in fear and dread, and therefore, we speak and live and act out of lack and desperation. In spite of our fear we commit to faithful convenant action and pledge to do justice amid the mysteries of life. We pray for the faith to live out our lives with You and with our loved ones in everlasting, life-affirming covenant.

Words of prayer comfort, console, and commend. Our words of faith bring solace and cheer in time of needed encouragement. We provide empathy and an understanding spirit. We praise God for all our blessings, choices, and for God's powerful presence within the lightning and thunder of the heavens or in the still, small voice, the majesty of new plant life, the laughter of children. We offer words of thanksgiving for the care and concern shown by loved ones. We tremble with fear as we think of what it means to be a responsible human being. We bless God for opening the doors of grace to us and for the opportunity to witness to others. We recognize those who have served faithfully in the past and in this present age for the salvation of all. We salute those who will work in the future for covenant faithful action. We rejoice for our rich heritage with God and for what can yet be. We note the grief and loss of the world when the covenant has been disregarded or abused by us. In all that is noble, just, true, and loving, we vow to be ever mindful of the potential of faithful covenant action as one approach to a beloved community.

Prayer of Commitment 3

Gracious God and Parent of Hannah, Leah, and Sarah, for all mothers who have been barren, for all those who have wanted to give birth to new ideas, new hopes and dreams, but who have felt sterile and empty, we call forth your mercy. Please give us that peace that passes all understanding that we might know those periods of quiet and emptiness are times to be still and to know that You are God, the giver of life.

We confess our faltering faith and ask that You shore us up in a manner that glorifies You on earth and in heaven. Help our unbelief and help us adjust to those moments when we feel alone, desperate, hopeless, unconnected with You. We desire to be more like You and recommit our lives to learning more about You and serving You in our daily lives as we meet our neighbors. Particularly as we meet those who are different from us, help us see Your beauty inside them.

We commit to being open for Your presence throughout the world. May we so focus our lives on You that even in the sterile, empty moments we will still know and honor You.

Life is full of experiences: some great, others mildly interesting; some thrilling and simultaneously frightening; and others simple and pleasurable. During the seasons of our lives, among continuums of change, elements of stability and surprise are important. In developing healthy communities of faith it is important to help participants understand that on any given day, change—often drastic change—may cause us to make decisions that we have never made before. In other moments of change we may feel empty and desolate like Hannah, wherein we bargain with God so that we might have a respite, a sense of relief. God has promised to always be with us, to never forsake us. Such a promise of intimacy and care is one not to take for granted or to minimize. Sometimes when a sense of barrenness overwhelms us we may have committed to too many tasks and may have lost focus or balance concerning our total health and well-being. Covenantal faith is a living faith. When we take faith seriously we are open to the renewing love of God.

Prayer of Commitment 4

As a covenant people, we pledge ourselves anew to being in relationship with God, the author and finisher of our faith. We take pleasure in God's love for us, and celebrate the ongoing prophetic tradition. We honor God's covenant that embraces the intimacy of worship and the passion for justice. We vow, Gracious One, to work for social justice causes on an individual level. When we stray from Your love and break our covenantal vows, please give us the strength to see our lapses and welcome Your forgiving love and grace in humility and joy.

We come before Your presence, sometimes with confusion and pain, sometimes with sadness, and usually with thanksgiving. Help us to be Your covenant people. By faith we acknowledge that You are the potter and we are the clay. You are the refiner even when we cannot love ourselves. By your grace we know we are being molded and fixed for the work of all that is blessed and good and loving and kind.

Words of prayer comfort, console, and commend. Our words of faith bring solace and cheer in time of needed encouragement. When we are attuned to God, we too can provide empathy and an understanding spirit. God calls us to a covenant of love, not a cauldron of misery. We need God's presence in our

71

lives so that we might experience the intimacy of covenant, knowing that we have a friend in Jesus. A friend can be an ally, confidant, assistant, helper, partner, alter ego, neighbor, patron, associate, colleague, crony, pal, playmate, companion, advocate, soul mate, defender, well-wisher, champion, or defender. Thus to know that we have a friend in Jesus is to be blessed, to know the intimacy of covenantal, embracing relationships. We transcend all emptiness, barrenness, and marginalization when we trust God's providential abundance. Ruth came from abundance. With the care and industry of Ruth, Naomi emerges out of her emptiness. With care and mutual support for one another, we too can know a faithful covenant of abundance that blesses us daily.

Chapter 4

Physical Health: Our Bodies, Our Temples

Made sacred; alive:
Divine Sculpting,
Divine Grace-filled Breath
Infusing cells, body and mind,
Soul identity,
Magnificence unbounded.

Births and deaths,
Love and laughter,
Family traits of height and girth,
Seriousness and mirth,
Eyes and hair and limbs,
Intellect and habits,
Legacies of DNA:
That signature won't betray.

Sacred flesh and blood,
Walking and talking,
Moving and grooving,
Singing and praying,
Temples embodying,
The pulse of life itself.

*T*he human body is a living, vital vessel magnificently created by God. Our bodies contain over 600 named muscles and
206 bones. Our brain, spinal cord, millions of nerves, and over
fifty billion other cells throughout our body make up our central nervous system, which controls our body. Our heart is a
muscle that contracts and relaxes about seventy times a
minute at rest, squeezing and pumping blood through its
chambers to all parts of the body by way of an amazing series
of blood vessels—a rubbery pipeline with many branches.

Strung together end to end, these blood vessels could circle the globe two and a half times. Our lungs contain almost 1,500 miles of airways, over 300 million alveoli, which process about thirteen pints of air every minute. Plants are our partners in breathing. We inhale air, use the oxygen in it, release carbon dioxide; plants take in carbon dioxide and release oxygen.[1]

Our physicality allows us to exist and be together in community, as opposed to being disembodied souls. The body is an extraordinary creation that serves us well when we take care of it. This divinely given instrument is a temple, a sacred house of worship, which we tend to take for granted and minimize its elegance, power, possibility, and nobility. The symmetry, balance of components, and the beauty lines bespeak the body's elegance. The strength, agility, and ability to engage in artistic movements—skating, basketball, ballet, dance, lifting, writing, painting, and playing musical instruments—indicate the body's power. The variety of shapes, colors, and sizes of persons that make up the human race signify the possibilities and nobility of individual and global community. Because the body is sacred, we have the remarkable ability to know consciousness and to love ourselves and others. So wonderfully made, the many functions of our bodies are self-contained and efficient. This magnificence of God, made manifest in the beautiful architecture of the human body, is vast. The creative spirits that exist and have existed through time emerge from the totality of ourselves. Our grace-filled bodies bring life, and when done, these bodies die no less sacred. Our bodies make the music of laughter and experience the animation of God's angelic chorus, singing together.

Meditations

Meditation 1

Seeing, touching,
Smelling, hearing, tasting,
Radiating energies of sacredness,
Speaking volumes
Of our souls.

These bodies of ours,
God's marvelous, majestic configurations.
Bombarding atoms,
Over the consciousness of time,
Grouped into families,
In love, in pain, in hope.

Moment by moment
Electric impulses
Feed the data of our hearts;
Stimulating our minds,
Nurturing our souls,
Caressing our bodies,
One sacred being, indivisible.

The two accounts of creation in the biblical text provide a poetic backdrop for heightening our consciousness about the blessed gift of our physical bodies and the marvelous, majestic design of these precious, sacred temples. Genesis 1 unfolds as God creates an orderly world from chaos and speaks everything into being within six days then takes a rest on the seventh day, the Sabbath. On the sixth day, God creates male and female in God's image, blesses them, gives them dominion over the earth, and pronounces *everything* created as good, including the physical body. The second creation story account follows from a different tradition and offers a different order of events.

This second creation story opens as the Lord God, Yahweh Elohim, creates earth, heavens, and waters for the whole earth. God, like a potter, then shapes and forms the male person "adam," the creature from the earth, "adamah," breathing into his nostrils, and the male person becomes a living being. Yahweh Elohim then creates a garden in Eden, with many trees, including the tree of life and the tree of the knowledge of good and evil. God gives the male creature free access to the garden with the exception of the tree of the knowledge of good and evil, and announces the creation of a helper as the male creature's partner. Yahweh Elohim creates every animal and every bird out of the ground and gives the male creature permission to name them and have dominion over them. Yahweh

75

Elohim puts the male creature to sleep, takes one of his ribs, closes that place up, and fashions a woman from that rib. In both stories the creation of humanity by the Divine expresses a dynamic orchestration of life, a picture of blessed benevolence.

Because of skewed theology many believe that the stuff of the body is evil because flesh is weak: this is a misinterpretation of the scripture, a denigration of a beautiful creation by God, and is problematic to any kind of redemption. To think that the flesh is inferior or the root of evil can induce a schizophrenic mind-set and rejects our sacred selves. To say that the body is not good contradicts the reality that we are created in the image of God, by God, given the belief that the character of God is good. That goodness manifests in some beautiful, awesome ways. The beauty of sight provides a panoramic view of all the world. The colors of bougainvillea and orchids, of sunrises and sunsets, of newborn babes and nodding older folk in the evening of their lives, of birds and bees, and of night and day provide us with a palette of memories. The beauty of sightlessness for the blind may heighten other senses or may hamper fulfillment. The blessedness of touch provides connection, sensuality, and consciousness. When touched in healthy ways, we know love, nurture, and comfort. When touched in ways that violate our personhood, we know fear, pain, and hatred for the perpetrator and ourselves. Divine touch, directly from God or mediated through an individual, re-creates and heals us.

The beatitude of hearing makes us familiar with melodic offerings of music, languages, noises, conversations, plays, poems, and broadcasts—sometimes a cacophony, sometimes distinct harmony. The beatitude of being deaf is the grace of privacy or the curse of secrecy. The blissfulness of taste is the joy of Epicurean delight, the gratitude for the privilege of having more than enough food. The curse of taste occurs when deadened taste buds can no longer relish the characteristic qualities of foods and drink or are defeated by anorexia or gluttony. The bounty of smell is the ability to appreciate the various aromas of foods, perfumes, flowers and tragically, the stench of pollution, toxic waste, and death. The benevolence of not being able to smell is the avoidance of foul scents, acrid or sour. The five senses are fine-tuned sensors that bring pleasure and completion to our lives and to the sacred moments of sensual experience.

Meditation 2

On wings of grace
We live and move,
Sing and laugh,
Dream dreams fantasizing,
Have visions mesmerizing,
Sharing bits of love.

We use our arms to hold and lift,
Bend and toss,
Swing across.
With hand and hand
We come to moments
of decision.

Our legs are gifts
That let us run
'Cross rolling plains,
God's great domains.
Wildflowers grow,
Birds soar above,
On wings of Grace.

The experience of flying is magical. A seemingly impossible possibility occurs when objects heavier than air are able to soar. The sons of a Methodist preacher had a vision that people could fly. Bicycle makers Orville and Wilbur Wright saw the splendid marvel of birds flying and dreamed they could invent a machine that would take human beings into the air. Today we fly daily with tons of cargo and people, throughout the world; we send astronauts into space beyond the earth's atmosphere. As we soar physically we are blessed to be able to soar mentally and emotionally within our imagination. We think and envision and remember through the marvels of our brain system, our intellect. This ingenious mechanism, our brain, designed by God, is the central repository of our own database; it controls the functions of our body. We think because of our sacred command center. Our brain allows for our consciousness and creativity, coordinates most voluntary movement, and controls and monitors our unconscious bodily functions like breathing and heart rate.[2] In acknowledging the sacredness of the body, we are better able to love ourselves.

One reason to treat the body well is because the body works well for us. We can lift and hold and bend and toss, run in fields and up stairs, and kick and jump and dance. We can hold and be held. We can sing and laugh and be affectionate. When we experience physical challenges and our bodies refuse to function well, we often feel betrayed. Some challenges are congenital; some are the results of poor health care, accidents, or environmental elements. The frailty of our physical bodies reminds us to embrace an attitude of gratitude for the services our bodies provide, and encourages a sensitivity to those who cannot take such things for granted. Such mindfulness invites us to regard the care of our bodies as an issue of faith: the context for being sensitive to the needs of those experiencing challenges; being sensitive in a way that affirms their reality without being condescending or offering pity. With covenant faith we realize that every individual matters and that we are called to love and respect everyone. Such awareness shapes what and how we eat, our attentiveness to hygiene and exercise, our attitudes regarding proper clothing; it makes us concerned about the amount of sleep and rest we get, and shapes our concern for the safety of our environments. Making our surroundings safe ensures that we are conscious of our language and thought processes, and that our buildings need to be accessible for physically challenged individuals. In faith we must become so conscious that we omit those attitudes and behaviors that rob others of their dignity. Most important, we must understand that an individual's challenged physical state is not the result of punishment by God of them or their ancestors.

Much about God and life is mysterious. Dispite our advanced technology and scientific discoveries in the twentieth century, we have yet to cure the common cold. Conversely, researchers are now working on using the cold virus as a carrier for a cure for AIDS. We have named many diseases for which we do not know the causes or the cures. We have learned the importance of washing hands, the use of antibiotics, and the importance of DNA in determining who and what a child will become in life. So much is unpredictable. Nevertheless, we can embrace the gift of our physicalness. We can take the very best care of ourselves as possible and make physical well-being an issue for our entire families. We can teach families and congregants to practice preventive health care, including the significance of eye and dental exams, physical checkups, healthy eating, exercise, and being aware of family health profiles as part of our faith practice.

Meditation 3

Open eyes,
Seeing mysteries;
The beauty, the sadness,
The puzzles of existence,
Trapped in the morrows.

Dear sacred ones:
Strong not invincible;
Muscles, tissues, cells,
Like a prayer,
Musical tapestries,
Ever sensual,
Move one to ecstasy.

Hallelujah Joy!
Feet of clay,
Withstanding tests of time.
Having borne thousands
From ship to shore
From east to west; Nine to five,
These weary travelers sustain.

Eyes, lenses that see and windows that afford insight into soul, are significant to our physical selves. When we use our eyes in meaningful, aesthetic ways, we experience profound insights and are privy to wisdom and knowledge. Often when we look we do not see, or see fully. We see either the trees or the forest, but not the trees and the forest. Sacred seeing is a way to appreciate the magnificence of God and God's creation as we value the privilege of being able to see with the physical, spiritual, or mental eye. What we see depends on when, where, and how we look and our various motives and reasons for wanting to see. Sometimes we do not see because we are not prepared or we have not been forthright in our presentation, as Joseph warns his brothers in their sojourn to Egypt (Gen. 43:1-8). The eye, like a camera, scans and takes in thousands of snapshots. Most camera eyes can discern the spectrum of colors. Persons who are color-blind may not be able to detect certain color distinctions, such as the distinction between red and green. Some of our camera eyes see colors but miss textures, distinctive dimensions, and shapes. Sometimes we look but have no desire to see. When we refuse to see the good, to see God, we begin to worship gods of stone and wood that have no redemptive power (Deut. 4:25). Sometimes people only see our weaknesses before we acknowledge our strengths, the very strengths that when known to our enemies become our weaknesses (Judg. 16).

The gift of sight opens up our world to know continuums—from beauty to ugliness, happiness to sadness, or existence to death. As we see, we gain knowledge and information (1 Sam. 23:23). Those who see without their physical eyes have a wealthy experience of our blessed, awesome, mysterious, elegant creation given to us by God. The Hebrew Bible understanding of *ra'ah* refers to the experience *to see,* both direct and implied. *To see* means to have an experience, to gaze, to take heed, to behold, approve, appear, or to view. Sometimes to see is to experience the affliction of others (Neh. 9:9), to no longer see that which is good (Job 7:7), to see someone's destruction (Job 21:20), or to see one's corruption (Ps. 16:10). Sometimes to see means to experience grandeur and beauty, the goodness of the Lord (Ps. 27:13). To see, one can know the love in the light of the Lord (Ps. 36:7-9), see the face of the voice of one's beloved (Song of Sol. 2:14), and the blessedness to the glory of the Lord (Isa. 39:2). To see is to encounter revelation, announcements, and disclosure.

The experience of seeing is a knowledge of reality, a perception of mundane and divine proportions. The Hebrew word *chazâh* means to gaze at, to perceive or contemplate mentally; to dream, to behold. This way of seeing is the act of beholding God while we are yet in our flesh (Job 19:26-27), an experience of a prophetic dream (Isa. 13:1), of having false visions (Isa. 21:29). When we look and desire to see, it is important to be prayerful and discerning.

In the New Testament, there are many terms—*optomai, diablepo, blepo,* and *eido*—that pertain to the act of seeing. *Optomai,* used in certain tenses, means to gaze with wide open eyes at something remarkable: the blessed see God (Matt. 5:8); one sees the heavens open (John 1:50); and when, through the power of the Holy Spirit, those who have never heard of Christ Jesus will see him (Rom. 15:21). *Diablepo* and its related *blepo* focus on the notion of to look at, behold, be aware, look (on, to), perceive, regard, see, take heed, to confirm through voluntary observation. When Jesus touched the eyes of two blind men, through their faith their eyes were opened. Sometimes those who have heard preaching and teaching see and hear, but do not perceive or understand (Mark 4:12). One can see through a mirror (1 Cor. 13:12), though the reflection may not be a clear image. One can, however, see with recognition (Eph. 5:15; Rev. 1:12). *Eido,* used in the past tense as a more mechanical, passive seeing, means to know, behold, be aware, perceive, be sure, or tell. One can see the light of God, of witness in others (Matt. 5:16), watch the process of events as they transpire (Luke 2:15; John 1:33), and observe, take note, or want to be in one's presence (Gal. 6:11; Phil. 2:28; 1 Thess. 3:6). To see, then, is to observe, to expand one's horizons, to encounter, to witness, to consider, to experience, to receive, and to understand.

Meditation 4

Hearing music,
Viewing heaven;
Smelling rosebuds,
Ambrosia oozing forth,
Tasting sweet elixers,
Mercy, life is good.

Palpating rhythms of life,
Touching hands together,
Caressing, hugging, loving,
Moments of intimacy:
Signifying Grace.

The largest mountain,
The infinitesimal nutria,
The whale and the mustard seed,
An ocean, a continent,
The great, the small,
All signify God.

Awesome wonders,
Physical splendors,
Intricacies and details,
Unimaginable connectedness,
Safety and health,
Relies on the breathing of us all.

Sometimes we experience lack and hurt because we live on the street of desperation, at the intersections of limits and unconsciousness. With the emergence of a new day we often fail to look and grasp its newness, its uniqueness. Sometimes our pains and angst looms so large that we cannot see the splendor in the grass or the twinkling of the stars. Prayertime can provide room for the shift from pain to appreciation. Prayer, human petitions to God or the Divine, as *t^ephillâh*, involves supposition, intercession, and is engaging (2 Sam. 7:27), a certainty that God hears and will deliver (Neh. 1:6; Isa. 38:5). Prayer may involve an imperative tone amidst a pressing awareness of distress (Pss. 4:1; 39:12), or a caution about who one prays for (Jer. 7:16).

Prayer, *proseuche*, involves praying earnestly, implies oratory, with a belief that prayer requested in faith produces results (Matt. 21:22), describes one of the functions of a temple (Luke 19:46), helps refocus a group toward unity (Acts 1:14), and is a means to overcome anxiety (Phil. 4:6). Prayer, as *deesis*, is a petition and supplication, for awesome blessings (Luke 1:13), shaped by one's heart's desire (Rom. 10:1), and is a vehicle of deliverance (Phil. 1:19). Prayer can give us clarity, a sense of well-being, and a heart more in tuned with God, in gratitude, intensifying our many senses. A stance of appreciation is an opportunity to see and hear and smell beauty; to know life as possibility, as good. Just as in seeing, hearing provides another modality for being with God. To hear, as *shâma*, engages the intellect toward obedience, discernment, and perception.

In the New Testament, *akono* denotes the ability to hear in various ways and to give or attend as an audience. When listening to parables as a keen observer of life, one who has ears ought to hear (Matt. 13:8*b*). One can also choose to leave when others refuse to hear (Mark 6:11). Part of the life of the faithful is to be supportive, to preach and teach so that others might hear and believe (Rom. 10:14). The Epistles reinforce a cautionary tale: we listen quickly, fastidiously, but speak and move to anger slowly (James 1:19). The gift of smell heightens our ability to interact with ourselves and our communities.

The experience of smell is closely related to the sense of blowing. *Ruwach* means to blow, to smell, to perceive in anticipation, to enjoy. Sweet smells of spices and frankincense are holy to the Lord and appropriate for worship rituals (Exod. 30:38). *Reyach,* related to *ruwach,* means savor, scent, smell. We can smell the smell of one's garments (Gen. 27:27), and we can smell with lovers delicious, intoxicating fragrances of bodies, ointments, and gardens (Song of Sol. 1:12, 4:10, 7:8). Sweet smells, such as freshly bathed and talcumed babies along with sweet smells exuding from kitchens, often provide comfort and signify an experience of nurture and love. Appreciating the sense of smell can serve as a warning or an invitation. Bad, virulent, gaseous, ammonia-like smells warn us of stress and unrest; good, sweet smells evoke pleasure and often relaxation. Relaxing is key to gaining pleasure from one's body and one's surroundings. Reckoning with or evaluating one's present reality from the context of sensitiveness and thankfulness opens up a new vista and a new way of seeing things that we often take for granted. Sensitivity to the inner connection of life helps us embrace the various rhythms that go on in our bodies and in nature. Awareness of these textures helps us celebrate our senses as we come alive, know intimacy, know God, and ultimately, begin to know ourselves.

Responsive Readings

Responsive Reading 1

Leader: Majestic sweetness is the sound of life itself. We honor God as we honor the blessed and sacredness of our bodies.

People: **Rejoice greatly, O daughters and sons of Zion; rejoice for the gift of health, for the gift of a body: to work, to play, to worship.**

Leader: Though we often take our bodies for granted, we know that all good and perfect gifts come from God.

People: **In Your perfection You give us excellence. We come in gratitude and praise for the amazing creation of our body: an extraordinary temple to house our being.**

Leader: From the beginning of time You pronounced us good. You created us in Your image: our bodies, our souls, ourselves.

People: **Fix our hearts and minds, that amid our frailness, we honor the blessedness of our temples and rejoice at the magnificence.**

Leader: We laugh, we sing, we celebrate our tallness and shortness; our slimness, our plumpness; our wrinkles, our smiles; our athletic abilities, our clumsiness; our color, our eyes; our noses, our ears; our limbs, our organs; our tissues and our muscles. Everything that comes together to form our physical selves we honor, we cherish, and we thank God for.

All: **Make us accepting of ourselves. Help us honor our bodies, care for our bodies, as they are our own temples.**

Much of our sensual experience is related to the sensitivity of sweet smells. Sweet smells signify one's ability to be holy and appreciative. Biblical mentions of smells relate to that which is holy: the pleasing of God or the pleasing of one's lover. When we embrace our physicality, the spaces where we live and all components of our daily lives as sacred, there is a greater chance for us to live a more balanced, invigorating, and healthy life.

Often assumptions that our flesh is weak, and therefore evil, have forbidden us from fully enjoying our physical bodies. We lose the ability to note the difference between the smell of perfume and that of room deodorizer. We fail to note that one of the reasons children have a musty odor after recreational activities is because they are healthy enough to run and play, and thus the body cleanses itself. As we better learn to pace ourselves and live in the present, we will have more times for discovery, to note the difference between the smell of roses and that of honeysuckles in bloom; the smell of what happens with garlic in Italian, Chinese, and Asian-Indian foods. At the level of smell, we can gain a whole new experience of God's wonderful world and the many people that dwell herein.

Responsive Reading 2

Leader: We laugh, we shout, we whisper and cry, we sing and moan. We delight in making angry, sweet, sad, and joyful noises unto God.

People: **We give thanks for the gift and blessing of speech. We recognize those that are mute, and know that we are made richer by the quietness that we all bring.**

Leader: We hear music and noise, great sermons and filibuster; a child's first words and the sweetness of choirs and symphonies.

People: **We rejoice that many of us can hear. We honor our deaf sisters and brothers as they hear in ways that we can only begin to imagine.**

Leader: We walk and run, wiggle our toes and bend our knees, we do sports and stand up tall. Such movement celebrates the grace of God.

People: **We thank God for the magnificence of our legs,** which carry us everywhere we go. We acknowledge those freed because of wheelchairs, walkers, and canes; who stand tall, even as they sit and lean.

Leader: We lift and type, write and crochet, cut and mend, paint and make gestures; we conduct orchestras and throw balls, and we touch.

All: We offer words of gratitude for movement and dexterity. We salute those in our commmunity who wave and work and gesture with their spirits and their voices. We rejoice for speaking, hearing, and movement.

The gifts of arms and legs, and what they can do, is tremendous. We watch in awe at the Olympic competitions as athletes throughout the world "go for the gold" in the summer and winter competitions. Some of their moves and acrobatics are mind-boggling and seem to defy gravity. Their polished routines are so magnificent that a child may say, "Look how easy they make that seem; I can do that." In the eloquence of physical awesomeness we see the simplicity undergirded by thousands of hours of practice, of financial investment, and of miles traveled to competitions. We see the simplicity of a loving Creator who has so magnificently made our bodies. We know the simplicity of the way arms and legs help propel us through space as we walk, run, climb, and stoop in our daily stream of activities. We know this ease as privilege, for many do not have the gifts of agility and movement. Many suffer from various forms of inflammation, nerve damage, and paralysis, which hinder their movements. With new technologies many of our sisters and brothers who are so challenged are free to move about and engage in many activities. We celebrate their being and their contributions to us, as they move and dance in their thoughts, their dreams, and their aspirations.

Responsive Reading 3

Leader: How delightful that we taste the sweet, bitter, salty; that we feel the textures of smooth, crunchy, feathery, tough, hot, and cold.

People: **We give thanks for the gift of taste and of meals to bring us together. We join with those who cannot taste, as children of God in solidarity.**

Leader: We see the clouds and rain, the birds and flowers, and the smiles and frowns. We see long lost friends and children's innocence.

People: **We celebrate the gift of sight; we embrace those who are without the gift of physical sight, and pray for those with sight who do not see.**

Leader: We recognize the blessings and the curse of a sense of smell. We enjoy, with balance, all pleasurable encounters.

People: **We pray for those with allergies and congestion, hindering their sense of smell: those that are pleasing or those that warn us of danger.**

Leader: O joyous grace, we applaud the talent and power of thinking, imagining, learning, creating, and remembering.

All: **We praise God for the gifts of thought and creativity; for the possibility of making a difference. We stand with those whose mental and imaginative faculties are challenged. May we embrace difference and acceptance; may we look in gentleness and not in scorn when we perceive someone as disfigured; and may we all know peace.**

Sometimes we get so caught up in our full schedules, our goals, and our aspirations that we forget the incredible capacity of our physical selves. We forget the amazing amount of information that our skin, our largest sensory organ, and all our other sensory organs take in and process during a given day. Getting in touch with our physical selves is an opportunity to celebrate our bodies, how our bodies serve us, and the sacredness of ourselves and all creation. The sacredness of these various facets of ourselves emerges from our createdness by God. Our bodies, as temples, are holy places, moving in holy spaces. Celebrating our sacredness means we eat and exercise properly, getting sufficient rest and relaxation. Celebrating our sacrality requires that we continue to learn about ourselves and our world, to know God's many glimmers of grace in our midst, and respect all with dignity. Practicing respect for others is a proactive way of minimizing hate and oppression in everyday ways in everyday places.

Responsive Reading 4

Leader: For taste, touch, smell, hearing, and seeing, we honor and glorify God. For movement, we offer thanksgiving. For the bounty of thought and imagination, we know joy.

People: **In thanksgiving and praise we shout Hallelujah!**

Leader: For the heart and our cardiovascular system that circulates our blood to our entire body, be grateful and keep your heart healthy.

People: **In thanksgiving and praise we shout, "Thank God!"**

Leader: For our lungs and pulmonary system, which filters out impurities, spreading oxygen throughout our bodies, be joyous and avoid carcinogens.

People: **In thanksgiving and praise we welcome God's mercy and generosity, Hosanna!**

Leader: For our reproductive and endocrine systems, which provide the systems for new life and balance in our bodies, be blessed.

All: **Allelulia, we are blessed with the amazing temple of our bodies.**

There are so many moments of blessed communion involved in the functioning of a sacred, human body. Such respect for the body is not idolatry. This kind of respect signifies and celebrates the magnanimity of God and our overwhelming privilege of having such extraordinary temples. When we come to realize our physical sacredness we begin to better know ourselves and experience incarnation. In those moments, where we are one with ourselves and thus experience a closer connection to all creation, we become fully embodied. The sacred becomes fully manifest in us and we know that we are *of* God. We realize that other persons—regardless of their age, gender, race, or sexual orientation—are also of God. Such experience is the beginning of our own transformation. We no longer grovel for power and subsist on greed, or manipulate and use others. There is no room in our world for oppression, hate, abuse; for lying, cheating, stealing, or misrepresenting ourselves or others. In those moments, we truly know God, ourselves, and our neighbors in a most profound way. We simultaneously know incarnation and resurrection. In those moments, we are free and wholly saved; justified, sanctified, redeemed.

Prayer of Commitment 1

Gracious, Loving God, we give You thanks for our bodies. You made us—wondrously, joyously. You gave us our bodies as gifts. In covenant faith, bless us with discerning joy that we might honor You, ourselves, and our ancestors by taking the best possible care of our bodies; that we not take our bodies for granted. Through the power of the Holy Spirit grant us the will to eat and rest properly; to exercise based on our physical and spiritual needs. Give us the wisdom to treat our bodies as holy vessels.

Help us embrace those who look different and who move in the world in ways different from us. Please quiet the hate we have for ourselves that we often project on others. Help us celebrate the artistry and grandeur of our physical selves.

As You give us food to eat and water to drink we stand in solidarity with the thousands who only know famine and who have no access to potable, safe water. Help us be better stewards of our natural resources. Let us be ever mindful that we do not live alone on this planet.

Conscious awareness of the physical body as sacred means that we pray differently. We pray with our whole selves. We come to hold our bodies differently. Our posture becomes more noble; our movement more gracious; for we cease to be imprisoned by external measurements and are empowered by internal peace. With the advocacy of the Holy Spirit, we embrace life in new and beautiful ways. Eating and sleeping become acts of spiritual care. Exercising, and reading inspiring texts, become integral to our spiritual discipline. We are empowered to make healthy choices out of affirmation and abundance. We are able to change negative habits because we now see the discipline of good self-care as grace. We realize that there is enough time, and that our time is better appropriated, when we share with those who are not as privileged as we are.

Prayer of Commitment 2

Blessed One, help us revere and respect the bodies of ourselves and of others. In anger and frustration we often lash out. Some of us let people use us as doormats and as whipping posts. Some of us spank children with slippers, belts, and switches, saying that we love our children, yet using violent acts for the sake of discipline, since this is the way many of us were disciplined. As such, we teach children that love is abusive and painful. Some of us use hurtful words that destroy the self-esteem of children, family, and neighbors. Show us alternative ways to love and discipline, so that we cease to ridicule and demean through speech. Help us know that we must not use fists, feet, guns, knives, or weapons against children, partners, spouses, and friends because we are afraid, because we think we are losing control, or because we crave power. Help us emerge from the haziness of denial and to learn how to communicate lovingly and to set boundaries for the health of all. Guide us so that we can teach and mentor with compassion so that we may become a true neighbor to others.

Our attitudes make an incredible difference in our perception and experience of our world. When our glass is half full we begin with advantage, hope, and possibility. When our glass is half empty we begin with deficit, pessimism, and dead ends. Many times the obstacle that stands in the way of our dream is our negative attitude: our thoughts of impossibility or of unworthiness. Somehow the thoughts become larger than life itself. The fear that becomes a cancerous thought is much more horrible than any scenario that could ever unfold. But it is the level of thought and its related attitude that crushes us. We unwittingly play into our own demise and destruction. But when we have "can do" attitudes and positive thoughts, even though we do not reach particular goals because of physical, emotional, and financial limitations, we can get close. With prayer, proper guidance, and support we can embrace the call that we know God has on our lives. Ultimately, happiness emerges in the manifestation of God's desire for us in our lives. God wants only the best for us; the desire of our hearts.

Prayer of Commitment 3

Merciful Spirit, often what we imagine we see is not what is truly there. Sometimes we think we hear that which was never uttered. Other times we imagine we would like to look different. Sometimes we become obsessed by dreams that may be unreasonable based on our DNA, our lifestyle, environmental factors, and the natural dimensions of our bodies, our temples.

Please give us wisdom concerning the precious offering of our physical body. Let us know that change requires an investment of time, perspective, and patience, and yet we may not achieve the results we expect. Give us a sense of balance and help us appreciate the blessed temples we have been given. Guide us in working with health care practitioners that we might experience health at its best. Let us resist the impulse to ingest things and to do exercises that will cause us harm.

Help us desire to be whole, well, and complete. Come Holy Spirit, help us know the blessing of our bodies. When we know illness and aging, bless us with dignity and peace. Bless us to love and be respectful to our bodies. Bless our community to surround us in love.

Each day that we live presents untold miracles. Babies are born and people, young and old, die. But in the dying they live, and in the living many die. Life, as an experience of worship, offers moments for worship, adoration, contemplation, listening, confession, and offerings. Each morning when we wake is the prelude, the introduction to the rest of the day. Our processional is the move from our beds to the other activities of our day. Our call to worship is a time of prayer when we recommit to living today with God. Our hymn of praise and all the music therein are the moments when we sing with our smiles and the good that we do to cheer on a weary traveler. The reading of the various scriptures is our actual time of Bible reading and reflection, and can prescribe how we read living texts—the people and events we encounter. Our giving of offering and tithes pertains to our orderliness in matters financial: being prompt in paying bills, spending according to our means, putting aside something for a rainy day, and sharing with those in need. Our hearing the sermon, the preached word, symbolizes those moments when we make conscious contact with God, to listen, be instructed and in tune with God and ourselves. The invitation to discipleship undergirds our day as we embrace the love of God in ourselves and in others. The benediction is our prayer time, at eventide, when we can rejoice and be grateful for the lives we have touched each day.

Prayer of Commitment 4

Holy, Holy, Holy God: You give us your sacredness in ourselves, for we are made in Your image. Teach us to treat our physical selves with care, like a prayer. In devotion, we whisper words of entreaty and words of faithful questioning, placing all our cares on the altar of life. Help us release our burdens that we may not be paralyzed by pain or grief. Teach us to know that to stand proudly with self-assurance does not mean that we are arrogant, and to love ourselves and our bodies is not an act of idol worship. Help us appreciate ourselves so that no garbage will contaminate our temples. We release verbal garbage, for we know we are not bound to or by gossip and negative information. Grant us peace in such a way that we have no need to fill ourselves with the wrong food, drink, or drugs. We release external garbage, which frees us from being party to, or a recipient of, any abuse—self-inflicted or from others. We are created as sacred beings; to live as though we are garbage is to live a lie.

The privilege of breathing in deeply is to experience the anointing of the Holy Spirit. We inhale the breath of God, the air God made, the air propelled through our bodies by God, knowing air is sacred and breathing is worship. A gift of this simple act is one we share with those blessed to breathe with ease. Yet many struggle and cannot breathe without support. Even in struggle, breath connotes life. Each moment that we inhale air and exhale toxins we have an opportunity to experience the anointing, when the spirit came down and all began to speak in diverse languages (Acts 2:1-4). Whether experiencing glossolalia or prayer language or the gift of speaking in everyday parlance, the Spirit of God gives each of us a way of speaking many different languages, of word, of body, of mind. God gives us the power of communication. We must be good stewards and honor our sacredness. Each breath, each cell, each impulse is sacred. To realize even an iota of the sacredness of ourselves means that we may know ourselves as incarnated love, peace, and contentment. When we know our sacredness we honor our temples. We become ourselves.

---

1. http//www.yucky.com/yucky
2. Ibid.

Chapter 5

Emotional Health: Love and Sexuality

Ooh, magic in my bones,
Hearts sing a symphony.
Energetic love potion,
Intimacies resounding,
God's celestial chorus:
Sing magnificently.

Hearts beating together,
Soul mates created,
Mirroring the twelfth of never.
Families springing forth:
Agape, Eros, Filia,
Multiple kinds of love.
Webs of wondrous affection, strung from:
Kitchen nooks and family rooms,
Front yards and Granny's swing.

Rainbows strewn across the sky;
Elegance in our babies' eyes;
Frailty when we take the first step.
In moments of discovery,
The ecstasy of giving and receiving:
Each moment we know love.

*L*ove and human sexuality make headlines, make billions of dollars for cinematographers and actors, are crucial to new beginnings, and make up the text of the most unread but most dicey book in the Bible (Song of Songs, Canticle of Canticles, Song of Solomon). Love makes Valentine's Day a hot-ticket item as millions buy cards, roses, and chocolates to send to a beloved. Love, and at the least, acts of human sexual intercourse, precipitate the births of thousands of babies each year.

94

Tina Turner's hit song "What's Love Got to Do with It?" turns all questions about love on their heads. We ask not only what's love got to do with it, but what *is* love? Love is one of those words that is easy to spell, often used too casually, and is difficult to define. Sometimes *love* is used to denote an endearment to a child. We use the same term to speak of adult intimacy. Love is a word used to describe the nature of one's delight in a job or hobby, or to describe our feelings about a sport, a season of the year, a facet of our lives, or a favorite food or drink. Such multiple uses of a word signal the complexities of the term, its meaning, its use, and its misuse. Depending on one's location, love involves power, joy, pain, ambiguity, hope, faith, loss, completion, disease, and health.

Meditations

Meditation 1

Mystical moments of bodies touching,
Smiling, holding hands,
Hugging and embracing: appropriately.
Joys of childhood,
Making mudpies, playing with wooden toys, creatively
When we don't believe in:
"I can't do that!"

Adolescents, laughing, playing, dancing,
Working to understand and be themselves:
A world of confusion,
Unbridled hormones,
Running rampant in their bodies.
As they are confused, nonplussed—changing,
Yet our children still,
Yet in need of love.

Who translates the tediousness of being a child?
Of being a parent?
Or growing older?
Who created the map,
That teaches how to play these roles,
Amid intense pain and pleasure?

New, confusing feelings,
Amid naïveté, young or old,
When others don't understand us;
When we do what we promised never to do,
What others have done.
Do we do the same,
When we want love
And don't know how to love?

There are many biblical terms that use the verb *to love* as a word that expresses an act, an occurrence, or a mode of being; as a noun or the name of something; and the experience of loving and being loved. The biblical concepts of love pertain to both divine and human love. *'Ahab* means to have affection—sexually and otherwise, as passion for a lover, unselfish loyalty for a friend, and steadfast adherence to righteousness. Such love concerns Moses' edict for Israel to love the Lord their God (Deut. 6:5); love as commitment of a lover (Judg. 16:15); David and Jonathan's mutual loyalty for each other (1 Sam. 20:3-4); and God's concern for justice (Ps. 97:10). *'Ahab* includes wisdom's affection and rewards to others (Prov. 8:17); the instances when God loves, heals, and restores (Hos. 14:4); and the declaration of love of one human being for another (Song of Sol. 1:3-4*b*). *Ahabah*, which tends to be exclusive,[1] relates to how one experiences love, and thus, how one intimately follows God's ways (Deut. 19:9). This love chooses, prefers, overlooks, is the preferential love by God for Israel, and relates to God's own jealousy (Exod. 20). *Ahabah* also refers to the deep affection and allegiance for a friend (2 Sam. 1:26); to the experience, sensations, and depths of human, sensual, sexual love (Song of Sol. 7:6, 8:4, 7); and to the ethical and spiritual requirements of love (Mic. 6:8). *Châshaq* means to take delight, to cling, have desires, and to possess the love of God through God's faithful assurance (Ps. 91:14). *Ra'yâh* conveys intimate relations with a female friend, lover, sister, companion (Song of Sol. 1:9; 2:10; 4:1; 5:2). Another mode of love, *râcham*, pertains to showing mercy, fondling, or having pity (Ps. 18:1).

In sum, love in the Hebrew Bible usually refers to a spontaneous, natural feeling, which moves one to self-giving or to grasp or gravitate toward an object that awakens such a feeling or to engage in an action where pleasure occurs. This love concerns the religious and theological, as well as the sexual and relational in families and friendships or masters and slaves. Shared human love is good. Biblical, sexual, erotic love is powerful. Love is a vital, ethical component to human life and community even though limits exist regarding love toward an enemy (2 Sam. 19:7). Steeped in covenant theory, love is actually not defined but is part of one's religious life, and is salvific. The love of God, with primarily national (Israel) dimensions, usually pertains to God's majesty, kindness, power, and authority rather than an attraction or inner feeling. In Deuteronomy, God's love concerns covenant and election—notably as a blessing for covenantal faithfulness.[2]

Agapao, to love in a moral or social sense, defines love for one's God and likewise, for one's neighbor (Mark 12:30-31, 33; Matt. 22:37, 39; Luke 10:27) and the experience of God's generosity and benvolence (Rom. 5:5). This understanding of love also reflects the arbiter of the faith (Gal. 5:6); the context for affection or the concern for others in the service of God (Phil. 2:1; Heb. 6:10); and the importance of having concern for God and humanity (1 John 4:20). *Agape,* affection or benevolence, relates to a love feast or a feast of charity; a fondness and kindness. One is admonished not to neglect *agape* for God (Luke 11:42) and is reminded that *agape* of God is to be within us (John 5:42). The greatest of the spiritual gifts (1 Cor. 13), *agape* is the catalyst for encouraging us to do good works (Heb. 10:24) and tells us how we are to be merciful to one another (Eph. 4:2). *Phileo* means to be a friend to, or have affection for (1 Cor. 16:22), especially for places of honor or for being seen (Matt. 6:5, 23:6; Luke 20:46).

Thus, in the New Testament, the most frequently used word for love is *agapao*, which for Jesus concerns will and action, when one lives in total faith, in God. The dangers to this love are mammon and vanity, the love of prestige, and the threat of persecution. Jesus demands that one love God, one's neighbors, and radically, one's enemies—not out of sentimentality or illusion, but out of reality. God's gifts of mercy and forgiveness, which embrace a sense of reconciliation, come with this new kind of love. Paul sees that the eternal love of God is embodied in the love of Jesus Christ, a life-changing event, which concerns the election or the salvation of God's chosen. Paul sees all of God's creation and redemption as the work of love that involves human participation and responsibility by faith. In the book of James, faith is love in action (James 2). In the Gospel of John, *agape* is the concept of the future, of the world of Christ, epitomized in the giving of the Creator (John 3:16); a revelatory, heavenly gift that triumphs through moral action.[3]

Meditation 2

A knowing look,
Or a gentle squeeze,
Connects us
With the loving essence of another;
One blessed, with whom we can commune,
If there is trust.

The times we share
Anniversaries and such,
Marking those moments
Celebrating the love:
Of committed partnerships,
Birthdays and accomplishments.
Families, extended and otherwise,
Together in sociability, in God.

A myriad of emotions follow us
In life and death,
In life cycles and disappointments:
We cry, we laugh,
We scream, we whisper,
About nonsensical things
Sometimes only pretending, in denial,
Feelings bubbling up,
Triggered by another's insensitivity,
A memory, a loss, a question.

There are many expressions of love, usually categorized as *filia, eros,* and *agape. Filia* denotes brotherly or sisterly care, concern, passion, and fondness. *Filia* involves great admiration, or care and commitment to associates and friends. Love for one's neighbor is one form of *filia.* Whether in fondness for an associate or a neighbor, such love is not entered into for the sake of gain, advancement, or self-aggrandizement. For any love to be genuine it must be free: freely given and freely received. Some people are incapable of receiving love—they feel unworthy or have very low self-esteem or have other issues that prevent them from receiving love. Some do not know how to love unconditionally for they themselves did not experience such unconditional love as children and have rejected themselves and others throughout their lives, in many ways, in an effort to prevent others from rejecting them first.

Eros is romantic and erotic love expressed between two persons involved in sensual and often sexual intimacy—ideally in a committed relationship; in a marriage. *Eros* relates to deep affection and passion, involving all the senses and a healthy appreciation for one's partner/spouse. Seeing the beloved other triggers the quickening of a heartbeat and brings delight. Touching that special person—from holding hands on a walk to sharing deep intimacies in bed—involves tactile sensations of the skin. Hearing the voice of the cherished other brings to mind memories of earlier special moments. Smelling that special cologne, perfume, or the essence of a romantic companion moves one to desire deeply. Tasting foods enjoyed by both, or the lips of that special loved one, can stimulate a physical erogenous zone that heightens the desire for intimacy. These feelings are natural and beautiful. Such shared passion in the context of a covenant commitment, and at its best a godly relationship, celebrates a sense that God has called each to be with the other.

Agape, one of the greatest expressions of love, is that experience of unconditional care and concern for others through the grace of God. *Agape* is love that God has for us and the type of love that is foundational for all healthy expressions of love. *Agape,* a freely given love, celebrates life, empowers all, and embodies generosity and care: an unselfish, energizing, embodied, incarnated love. One of the supreme examples of *agape* is that manifested in the revelation of Jesus Christ. Such embodied love meets people where they are and ministers to them, creating an intimacy, a spiritual oneness. *Agape* shared between God and humanity is powerful as it affords an incredible sense of peace, contentment, and joy even amid difficulty and loss. Such love engenders faith and hope: an undying trust and a fervor for possibility.

Meditation 3

Couples walked along
As the tides rolled in
Sun set and day became night
Amid all the days of their lives
As first meetings became anniversaries.

Their passions steamed the windows
As their sensuality and desire
Intensified to moments of highest liturgy,
Hence bells tolling and choirs singing
As together they know each other
And they become one.

What majestic sweetness
Embraces them in their knowingness.
Celebrating the awesomeness of God
Who spoke all creation into being.
The glory of this heightened spiritual moment
Is itself one fullness of Sacred Joy unfurled.

The holiness of love:
Expressed with bodies,
Extolled in song and poetry,
Emphasized in Dance,
Enlightened through peace,
Embraced by God.

People make lifelong commitments in all kinds of partnerships at various times. Some people get along so well that in early childhood they commit to an adult partnership together and years later they become partners. Some teens meet, proclaim their love for each other, and marry soon after they reach eighteen. Others commit to each other in various ways at some point then go their separate ways, only to return to each other later in life. Then there are others who are not equipped to be in relationships of mutuality, kindness, good faith, and trust. Such persons often end up in dysfunctional relationships constructed on denial and sustained on a pathology, illness, or disease. Just as some people do not honor their physical bodies and health, others do not even consider their emotional life until a crisis occurs. When illness strikes, when misunderstandings occur, and obsessive-compulsive behaviors run amok, life situations become very tense. Such tensions are an opportunity to pull together as a community and to love one another well toward healing.

Healing is a process for people who want to get better. With issues of emotional health, mental anguish, or matters of the heart, the first steps involve the recognition that something is wrong. Some thrive on denial and "let's pretend that nothing is wrong." However, if we assume that nothing is wrong, then we believe that everything that occurs within a relationship is fitting. After admitting that all is not well, it is important to be willing to get well and to do the necessary work to affect healing. Following a proper diagnosis and a core plan of action, the individual, and in most instances the entire family unit, will require treatment. When one person is ill or the adult family members have been living in a sick relationship, the entire family may have adopted their behavior and made concessions in their relationships. Part of the holistic healing process requires a reorientation of all family dynamics and interactions, especially in long-term dysfunctional family situations. Some family members will not make the transition easily or willingly.

Meditation 4

Depression, like a distant thunderstorm,
Looms upon the horizon
Of our minds, and of our bodies;

Such heavy blankets.
That shroud our minds,
In the struggle to become whole and sane.

Our minds and psyche,
Often tormented and conflicted,
Sometimes congenital, sometimes environmental,
Sometimes chemical, sometimes event-oriented.
The madness that pains us;
And people name us crazy.

Some say: "Get over it."
"Just put your will to it."
"You can overcome it."

Nature's uncertainty and origins of "it"
Make "it" no less life-threatening and dangerous.
Emotional and mental illness
No cause for shame or blame;
No cause for fear;
An impulse for care.

Mental and emotional illness
Are amazing albatrosses.
Bogging one down behind drawn curtains,
In a malaise of prescription drugs,
That slow down, speed up,
Have side effects,
Make one old;
Easy to discard.

The song "Love Is a Many Splendored Thing" reminds us how complex love can be. Often we give love or at least attention to others but cannot love ourselves. To avoid the rejection that we sense will automatically come with intimacy, we dump and dismiss others before they can reject, dump, and dismiss us. We are abrupt, rude, or in some way dispicable so that other people will not want to be bothered with us. We wear the cloak of "the victim" well. Sometimes people cannot experience love because of underlying reasons such as depression. Some of us are depressed and have felt down for so long that such feelings are normal for us. Some depressions are situational. The pressure, confusion, or stress of our lives gets so out of kilter that our systems shut down in order to survive. Many times we do not see any options and we forget that we made some of the choices that have resulted in our dilemma. In most decision making there is some leeway. Once we have set certain actions in motion and we find that this may not be the best possible solution, we need not remain victims of our own making. We can change our decisions and our mind-sets.

One philosopher, economist, and devout Christian[4] has developed four freedoms: (1) the freedom to say no; (2) the freedom to say maybe; (3) the freedom to change one's mind; and (4) the freedom to make a mistake. A holistic approach to life and salvation could certainly incorporate these freedoms as an alternative to being trapped and becoming angry at oneself to the point of embracing destructive behaviors. Other depressions can result from a chemical imbalance in the body where all the right planning, goal setting, and willpower will not and cannot have a lasting impact on how one experiences oneself or others or the world.

Unfortunately, there is often a stigma attached to having a mental or emotional illness or disorder. We rally for accessible buildings for the physically challenged. Taking medication and changing one's routine of diet and exercise to deal with high blood pressure or diabetes are applauded and encouraged. However, in instances of mental and emotional trauma, we tend to want "those people" to vanish from our everyday life, to go away to a long-term care facility. We are uncomfortable with mental illness. God's created order involves a cornucopia of persons on the continuum and some are the extremes of mental and emotional health. We have an opportunity to encourage others to seek appropriate medical help, to advocate for adequate health care, and to love our friends and family, giving them room for self-discovery and an environment of honesty where they get support for health and life issues without condescending or judgmental attitudes. In these moments our best gift can be that of listener-advocate.

Responsive Readings

Responsive Reading 1

Leader: Rejoice for love, faith, and hope abounds. Love creates a foundation for growth, nurture, and health.

People: **Rejoice, O children of God! We are miraculously, wonderously made. God gives us the gift of love as a healthy way of being in the world.**

Leader: Sing songs of love in your gestures and words to the one who is lost, saying: God cares, God loves you.

People: **O God, fix our hearts that each heartbeat brings us closer to You, and creates a rhythmic tune of compassion.**

Leader: As Mount Zion rejoices we daily worship and give thanks for Divine blessedness and unconditional love, for ourselves and others.

People: **Gracious One, fix our ears and tongues that we hear and speak with discernment, as we live the gospel of sound mental and emotional health.**

All: **In thanksgiving and hope we support mental and emotional health. We move to do justice, love mercy, and walk humbly with our God.**

What a gift of blessedness to know love, the greatest spiritual gift, as the basis of one's moment-to-moment existence. What if every time someone wronged us we were so conscious of living amid the love of God that we could in that moment both pray for the individual and remove ourselves from harm's way? What would happen if we so radiated the love of God that persons in pain would first be attracted toward that grace and would not need to attempt to destroy us? Such love is available to us if we are open to such transformative power. Such generous love can serve as a catalyst for the awakening, encounter, transformation, and ongoing healing and health of others, rekindling the possibility for a fulfilled, spiritual life—our heritage from God.

One of the most repeated commands in the New Testament is the command: "Love thy neighbor as thyself" (Matt. 5:43, 9:19, 22:39; Mark 12:31, 12:33; Luke 10:27; Rom. 13:9; Gal. 5:14; and James 2:8). This command is also found in the Hebrew Bible in Leviticus 19:18. This major command of the Christian religion is second only to the command to love God. However, many people exclaim, "How can I love a Charles Manson or a Ted Bundy?" The answer is deceptively simple. This simple command requires that we "give *our* love to our neighbor," no matter how unworthy that neighbor may seem. This command demands that we first find love in ourselves, and then give that love to ourselves—no matter how unworthy we seem to be. Once we have given love to ourselves, we must then give that love to every other human. There is also a paradox in the Bible: if we are unable to give love to a fellow human—whom we can see—then is it possible for us to love God—whom we cannot see?

Responsive Reading 2

Leader: God's love created humanity in love as good, endowing us with ideas, thoughts, emotions, and feelings that move us to share our love.

People: **Blessed be the love of God, the force of all life, strength, and pleasure. Such gifts call us to act responsibly toward the well-being of ourselves and our communities.**

Leader: Our thoughts are the germs of new ways to live, be healthy, and grow. Our emotions temper our thoughts toward joy, peace, and affection.

People: **Blessed be the peace of God for serenity and balance in the fullness of our lives and our relationships, in a life of faith, as sensual, sexual beings.**

Leader: Experiencing feelings of intimacy, mystery, and hope in all relationships, we ask for the grace to reflect God's vast respect for all humanity.

People: **Blessed be the joys of God, incarnated in our experiences of touch, taste, hearing, sight, and smell, as beautiful, beloved creatures called by faith.**

Leader: As God gives us life, God gives us the abilities and talents to create marvelous ways of thinking about existence and about living in the world.

All: **Blessed be the faith of God, that abiding, eternal concern for humanity, which encourages us to live out a life of trust and hope, celebrating emotional and mental health, of love and sexuality, as we go forth to spread God's message of love.**

To experience God's love as blessing, as the controlling factor in our lives, is to know life as consecrated, honorable, and joyous. Such love makes all that we say and do as sacred as an act of worship. Do we sometimes fail to maintain this element of holiness in our coming and going? Certainly, but when we are conscious of the availability and the richness of living in this web of ecstasy we will always have hope and can situate ourselves and shape our lives to come close to this experience of love. A notion of life as sacred means we are always in close proximity to God. We can also see divine magnificence in soaring birds, in blooming flowers, in the formation of granules of sand, in the rays of the rainbow, in the smiles of children and youth, in the shared glances of couples, and in the wisdom of those graced with longevity. In those moments we know the extraordinary, but more important, the ordinary manifestations of God.

Responsive Reading 3

Leader: We stand in God's presence, in gratitude for the beauty of the human body and spirit, as vessels of elegance, not shame.

People: **As people of God, we claim our blessedness and reject the negative descriptions of humanity as central to our makeup and instead see that we are created in God's image.**

Leader: We celebrate God's presence in us by living a life of justice, sharing, and community where none are demoralized.

People: **As people of God, we accept our relationship**

with God as an act of worship. We endeavor to live mindful of who God created us to be.

Leader: We recognize that daily some people do bad things. Daily, many people are victims of abuse. Daily, hundreds of people do marvelous acts of kindness.

People: **As people of God, we pledge to do what we can to curb abuse. We pledge to do random acts of kindness.**

Leader: We honor the beauty of humanity and the awesomeness of healthy God-given parental, familial, neighborly, sensual, romantic, and sexual love.

All: **As people of God, we stand in awe of the opportunity we have for growth; we look in amazement at how well we have loved; and we listen, in humility, for the ways we can be more respectful and caring for all life and realities on our planet.**

On many days, many of us get so caught up in the minutiae that we miss the big picture and the little blessings. On other days, some of us are so ensnared in pain that we hardly ever experience a quarter of the love our friends and family want to share with us. Others of us are terrified of being loved. Our armor is so thick that we physically repel love. Some of us forget that today is the tomorrow that we feared yesterday. In this today we have an opportunity to pray for the willingness to love and be loved. We have a chance to spread enough love so that we can help provide an option to violence. We can begin by watching what we say and how we speak. Sometimes a retort or nasty reply makes matters worse. Sometimes we need to call a time-out and go away to reflect. With more openness and a willingness to have everyone be well and healthy, we will develop new options to live violence-free and have more positive experiences of parental, familial, neighborly, sensual, romantic, and sexual love, as we fulfill our commitment to God.

Look to this day,
for it is life,

The very life of life.
In its brief course lie all
The realities and verities of existence,
The bliss of growth,
The splendor of action,
The glory of power—

For yesterday is but a dream,
And tomorrow is only a vision,
But today, well lived,
Makes every yesterday a dream of happiness
And every tomorrow a vision of hope.

Look well, therefore, to this day.[5]

Responsive Reading 4

Leader: When we look at each other, we stand in the presence of the Divine. As we interact with others, we know God's faithfulness and mercy.

People: **As thinking and loving creatures we sometimes err and cause harm. We invite God to fix our hearts that we may love more and hurt less.**

Leader: Just as God said, "Let there be," and creation came into being, God calls us to live, "let there be peace and love in community."

People: **As thinking and loving creatures we know God has no eyes but our eyes, no hands but our hands, thus we are to do God's justice work.**

Leader: We know that God made us marvelously well, and we celebrate that our minds, bodies, and spirits are beautiful and equally of God.

People: **As thinking and loving creatures we tend to separate our bodies from our minds and our spirits. By God's grace we are functioning as one.**

Leader: We recognize our bodily sacred temples given in trust. We will be vigilant to assure that no one abuses, persecutes, or takes advantage of any child or adult.

All: **As thinking and loving creatures we accept the responsibility for creating healthy communities. By faith we will no longer allow domestic violence, incest, or sexual exploitation to remain silent bullies in our homes, our congregations, or our communities.**

Some of us fear new knowledge and new experiences. We are racist, sexist, classist, or have horrendous phobias because we are terrified of people who look, think, or act in ways that are different from our own. This fear, and often ignorance, is so thick that we forget God made that person too. At the juncture of seeing and thinking, our minds go blank toward new possibilities and our minds retrieve the garbage we were taught, we read, or we overheard. Fear and ignorance can be a deadly combination. Taken together, both often result in prejudice, hate, and war. What a pity that most of our global wars are the result of money, belief systems, and power structures: religion, politics, and culture. Whether we are talking about the Montagues and Capulets of Shakespeare's "Romeo and Juliet"; the Serbs, Croats, and Albanians of Kosovo; the Israelites, Egyptians, and Canaanites; or the domestic issues of gang warfare, hate crimes, and glass ceiling culture in the United States—the issues remain the mix of stereotypes, ignorance, and power. If we can begin to see the divine when we look at one another wherever we go, we can begin to live a life of mercy and faithfulness. When seeing and believing occur in the context of blessing, we begin to be fully human. We become open to a deeper experience of the sacred.

Prayers of Commitment

Prayer of Commitment 1

Holy One, majestic and loving Creator of all: we have few words that fully express our deep appreciation to You, for the genius present in the creation of humanity and of the world. Each day we call

> *You blessed and give thanks. For the beauty of love and the power-ful feelings that emerge in the rituals of courting, commitment, marriage, aging, giving birth, and of deep friendships, we give thanks. We appreciate those who choose to be single and have full and complete lives and a host of friends. We celebrate and honor those who have been adopted and those who have adopted children. We salute foster parents and all the unnamed, unsung persons who take time to listen to children and adults—affirming, loving, and guiding in noninvasive ways.*

> *Gracious God, for the lives of all persons in caring relationships, we give thanks. For the beauty of the five human senses and the abundant joy they give us, we offer gratitude. As we learn to treat our physical, mental, emotional selves as sacred vessels, help us support others in doing likewise. We pray for the transformation of those beings who need to hurt others, that they might see their wrongdoing, seek help, atone for their ills, and become healthy, respectful members of our communties.*

When we accept that God is love and that as children of God we embody love, life itself takes on new meaning. We come to a realization that there are many ways of living, and many healthy ways that families can exist. We also realize that there have never been any "good old days." One can only subscribe to that adage if one lived a life of privilege, deaf to total lived society. In the United States, and throughout the world, there have always been drugs, and except for very few pockets of geographical terrain, there has always been war. Violence has existed for far too long. Our awareness or lack thereof is a product of how much we have read and listened. MTV and current films are not the sole genesis of violence in media. The majority of operas, Chaucer's *Canterbury Tales*, many of the plays of Shakespeare, and all of the Greek tragedies are rife with explicit sex and explicit violence. One difference is that the media of written texts leaves more of the violence to our imagination. The moment violence is cast in live action and entertainment is the moment the intensity often increases. We can be aware of this violence and vow to see if we are either perpetrators or silent witnesses to acts of violence by others. We can listen better and be proactive in creating environments where we experience humanity as sacred, where we help ourselves and others find professional help early on, working toward reducing the daily outpouring of violence on those God has created sacred.

Prayer of Commitment 2

We praise You, Great Shepherd and Midwife of us all, for Your wondrous love, Your mercy and kindness. We pray that You help deliver us from our sense of shame and ignorance about our bodies, minds, and spirits. Some of us have been taught and have come to embrace ignorance when it comes to who we are and why we are here. We invite You to begin to bring us to a point where we can see the mistakes and our narrow thought. As we grow and develop, please give us the ability to see and to live our lives as your sacred ambassadors for peace and community.

We embrace Your new revelations and the joy that comes from unconditional love. Help us move with integrity and an openness to sharing Your love with others. We lift up our hearts for an infusion of Your grace. We lift up our bodies to be consecrated anew to Your service, that we may honor our own bodies and those of others, respectful of boundaries and mindful of the need to hold and be held in appropriate ways. We open up our minds and our spirits to be stregthened and flooded with Your peace, faith, and desire to be in joyful communion with others as sacred vessels called by You to do ministry in common and uncommon ways.

Every moment of every day, God is creating and inspiring us to create. Moments when we feel bored are opportunities to experience gratitude and to go and help someone else. Just as God cares for us in so many ways, we are to be the hands, ears, and eyes of God so that other moments of creation and recreation can occur. When we assume the role of learner we will see so much more. Life is so complex that no one individual can grasp its entirety. God wants us to appreciate the complexity as an opportunity and a call for us to be in community. Complexity is an invitation for collaboration. Together we can be partners with God in making a difference. Whether age two or ninety-two, we can learn from one another: how to treat one another better, and how to better take care of ourselves.

Collaboration with others means that we will come into contact with folk who can do some things better than us and some folk who we can do better than. When we come together in faith, we can learn to appreciate differences and to agree to disagree without anyone losing face or without becoming lifelong enemies. Collaboration that begins with gratitude involves moments of transformation and love.

Prayer of Commitment 3

God of the mountains, of the covenant, of Hagar, Josiah, Mary Magdalene, of Phoebe, Julia, and Timothy, of all those saints of the early church, we honor You and rejoice for the blessedness of all the earth. We bless You and ask that You remember us in the days of our youth and old age as we honor the sacred bodies, minds, and spirits that You gave us. Help us honor our total selves in practical ways. Give us the courage to eat and exercise properly, to read and listen in ways that are stimulating and healthy for our minds, to maintain a spiritual discipline and practice that will nurture our spirits.

Gracious One, on You we must rely. You have made us so magnificently that we want to honor the gift of life as embodied persons. Help us take the time to pray, to sleep, and to relax as spiritual practice. Teach us to pray in a way that we remain open to hearing Your voice. Help us sleep and rest deeply in You, that when we awake, we do so with anticipation. Help us be open to the healing needed when we have been abandoned, betrayed, or crippled by the mean words and acts of others. Help us challenge systems of oppression, that they might be changed for the glory of God and all of God's creation.

We live on a planet millions of years old that each spring brings forth new life. There are so many ways in which we can experience nature and its beauty, and as human beings we have taken liberties with other living species and with the waters and soils on planet earth. We have constructed buildings and bridges, have mined for coal, and drilled for oil and diamonds. The gift of having dominion over the earth comes with the responsibility of being good stewards. Each of us must daily assess what we do and how we do so. We honor

God by taking good care of all creation. We also honor God when we treat each and every aspect of our lives as sacred. If there are things in our lives that we do not feel ought to be treated in a sacred manner, then perhaps this part of our lives is not necessary. If we cannot do it in love of ourselves or our neighbors, perhaps this is a habit better left undone. When everything is done in the context of the sacred, we have an opportunity to really see as God invites us to see. There is a good chance then that we will end up taking better care of ourselves, understanding that as sacred vessels we deserve the appropriate amounts of sleep, food, work, play, worship, and rest.

Prayer of Commitment 4

O Giver of Life, master composer, architect, and designer of the universe, we come in humility and anticipation, for You only are God and we are Your children. We come mindful that You care, not because You have to care, but because You want to care and because You love us so much. Help us desire to love You, ourselves, our families, and our friends. Help us be vessels overflowing with the love appropriate to share in each of our relationships that we might be examples to those who do not know how to love. As we get closer to You, help us be mindful of those who yet strive. Help us have the room for those who falter. Help us have the courage to say and live No! to abusive language, thoughts, and acts. When issues of violence and abuse arise, help us provide an environment where others will see their wrong and seek the help needed to end their misbehavior. As we honor You, help us honor Your total gifts of spiritual, familial, sensual, and sexual love. Help us be romantic through all seasons of our lives and never tire of showing our love for others. Help us be sensitive to the needs of others in a healthy manner where they will never tire of being with us and loving us. Help us bless our families and our communities embracing Your love in a manner that is life-giving, life-affirming, toward total salvation and liberation.

As we are blessed to become older, we come to realize that our vision of God has changed. We no longer look for God to be a Santa Claus whom we focus on only once a year, but for a God who is vital in our daily lives. Even then, we often limit

113

our experience of God, for we limit our prayer time and our imagination toward the various ways God can be real in us. When we open ourselves for God's love, we become more aware of how God sends us glimmers of grace. We begin to see the embodiment of God in the little, ordinary things people say and do. We begin to embrace the presence of God in movies, poetry, and song; in smiles, embraces, and handshakes. Because God created us all and we are created in God's image, the more we have a God-sense the greater the sense of God we experience. These revelations concern our own awareness. God is always present, our connections are hampered or faint. Each moment serves as a reminder even in people we do not like. As our God consciousness increases, so does our peace, serenity, joy, and sense of community; so does our capacity to experience love in its many splendoredness.

---

1. Gerhard Kittle, ed., *Theological Dictionary of the New Testament*, vol. 1 (Grand Rapids: Eerdmans, 1964), 38.

2. Ibid., 23, 28-34.

3. Ibid., 44-53.

4. My husband, best friend, and partner in life's ventures, the Honorable Michael A. Kirk-Duggan, Emeritus Professor, University of Texas at Austin, developed these four freedoms toward achieving a balanced, healthy, and faith-based life, cf. *The Grapevine*, January 1984.

5. Sanscrit proverb by Kalidasa, an Indian poet and playwright, fourth century C.E. Richmond Walker, *Twenty-Four Hours a Day*, rev. ed. (Center City, Minn.: Hazelden Foundation, 1975).

Chapter 6

Spiritual Health: The Integrated Self

A sigh, a stretch,
A twist, a turn:
I feel me totally connected.
My majestic body,
Given me by God.

My capstones,
Spirit and mind
Working together:
I know, feel; think and emit;
Create, cry; imagine and fret;
My body knows lots of data
Flooding my system.

Sometimes I want quiet
To buffer the rich cacophony of
People, places, things—all register,
As I deeply cherish,
And sometimes belittle,
Others, in God's created order.

Phew! Awesome!
Thoughts, ideas, feelings;
Wrapped in my logic,
Shaped by the incredible Grace of God,
Which spins and welds my soul.

Rejoicing, I stop stretching,
Only to smile, and know
When the Great One spoke,
Created me and thee,
And named us Good!

*W*hen we live in present time, conscious of the blessedness of each moment, we are open to different ways of seeing, hearing, and thinking. We know the brilliance of divine construction, the elegance of life, and the exhilaration of discovery. In seeing the intricacies of divine architecture we get to appreciate the continuum of nature—from steep mountain ranges to the fragile jelly fish, from the miracle of birth through the ambiguity of adolescence to the complexities of aging. If we say *Yes!* to a life of faith as the context for our spirituality and health, we begin to appreciate the times and seasons of our lives. We embrace each day as a work of living art, with the symmetry of time and life cycles, framed by divine love. To achieve a sense of balance and an appreciation for life, health, and faith requires work.

A vibrant faith must be nurtured. Such trust grows with diligence and spiritual discipline, where one takes the time to connect with God, study scriptures, meditate, and listen for God's reply. So often we are on a treadmill of packed schedules and megastress. Everything is due two weeks before yesterday. Our schedules are so full that we often do not sleep well or rest deeply. We cannot turn our minds off. Spiritual health involves an integrated experience of body, mind, spirit, and spiritual practice, moderation in most things, and an attitude of irrepressible joy.

Meditations

Meditation 1

A spirited joy in my heart
Sings a symphony, a blues tune,
Some R & B, an aria or two,
A hymn my parents taught me,
Possibly rap or country, too,
'Cause I can: celebrate my joy.

My soul and your soul,
The inner parts of us,
That pull us together,

116

Hundreds and thousands of beloveds
Connecting, moving, loving,
Challenging, thinking,
Unless some Grim Reaper
Comes too soon,
'Cause someone blew us away:
Literally or actually.

Either way death—
Corpse or the walking dead—
Need not happen,
When we know God,
And know ourselves.

Then we know peace and serenity.
Not envy; no need to get stressed out.
No free rides,
And we need not get confused
About that which is simple: Love.

Love wants for nothing;
Love wants no pain or grief.
If love hurts,
The hurt comes not from love,
But from spite and misunderstanding.

As opposed to exploring specific biblical terms, in this chapter we examine thematic developments, particularly investigating those three texts that we identify as Wisdom literature: Job, Proverbs, and Ecclesiastes. *Wisdom* is a modern term used to designate a type of writing that emerged in ancient Israel and the ancient Near East. Wisdom concerns a way of life, a way of understanding the world. The concept of order is found in this Wisdom category. This ordering allows one ultimately to understand life itself despite the injustice, apparent confusion, or disorder. Wisdom shows the connection and distinction between wisdom and prosperity and between folly and destruction. The Wisdom adages can be short, pithy, concise statements or long poems.

Theologically, the Wisdom motifs connect God, the source

and guide for human life, with order and community. The sayings are speculative, pragmatic, or practical. The world is humanity's home. Significant issues are justice, mutuality, truth, consistency, and power. Thus life makes sense and has a definite meaningful order. The character of God's mind and will, together with the meaning or the reality behind the world, are the same: order, goodness, and meaning. In this context the goal of human existence is a healthy community life. How does one know how to live? One can trust experience. Because life is entrusted to humanity, we are called to be responsible stewards. Being responsible allows one to celebrate, enjoy, and share life and the world. From this viewpoint God is constantly present to nurture, support, and facilitate the wholeness of life.

Wisdom can help us sort through our perceptions, goals, attitudes, and sense of God, for an "integrated self" needs to resonate with biblical and conventional wisdom. Often we do not understand the ways of God or the way life unfolds. The death of a single child—from Sudden Infant Death Syndrome or from being hit by a drunk driver—has no logic or beauty, and saying, "It must have been God's will" seems perverse. Certainly families look for reasons and for someone or something to blame. Many times the only way people can live through tragedy without going insane or becoming catatonic is to claim that this misfortune was God's will. If one ascribes benefits and grace to a good, benevolent God, how could such a God exact such pain? These are the moments in which the wisdom of Ecclesiastes, in realizing that some of life remains mystery, is helpful. Similarly, Job reminds us that we will not always get the answers to our questions about life and that many life circumstances are not fair; further, we have choices to make about what we do and how we perceive our experiences. Proverbs provides short, pithy sayings that do not always work in contemporary life, but many provide an adage that serves as a reminder for attaining balance in one's life.

One can take comfort in knowing that there is order behind life. This awareness provides a context for encouraging us to be disciplined and balanced, and to embrace the wisdom of those who have come before in a way that celebrates them and helps us be more balanced with a life of ethical integrity. The elders can teach us that we can have vocations without being enslaved, without sacrificing our health and family relationships, aware that there are consequences to our actions or inactivity.

Meditation 2

God's image, in you and me,
In spirit and love, combined.
The radiance of the impossible,
The delight of the irrepressible,
Joy and peace incomprehensible.

Your spirit, my spirit, our spirits,
Mingling, making community,
Contributing to the wellness
Of the whole people,
Multiplied and divisible,
By the Oneness of God.

Spirits, like blood, are real—needed
For wellness and health.
Healthy blood flows and brings forth new life,
Dead or diseased blood brings death.
Healthy spirits flow and generate pliancy and hope
That refuses to die, even when the physical body
Returns to dust,
Wounded spirits, like dead blood, emanate death.

O Jerusalem and Mount Zion,
The City of God meets our temples:
Healthy spirits and bodies and minds working together,
Creating Cities of God,
Where our lights shine and illumine
In Ethereal majesty—
Godly nobility—
The City of resurrection and eternal life now.

There are days when even the bluest sky, a sense of thanksgiving and gratitude, and a knowing that others love us are not

119

enough. There are many pulls on our lives and sanity. Many issues that seem important to our well-being, seemingly the desires of our hearts, arise. Sometimes it seems that the obstacles are too great and the resources too few for us to accomplish the good that we want for ourselves and others. Those are the days when focusing on God may be the best that we can do. Such times are painful and require that we "let go and let God," and live in the moment. Being stuck in what happened yesterday and worrying about what might happen tomorrow serves no good purpose. More important, we miss the blessings of today. We miss the opportunity to work constructively and to make a difference where we can.

Discomfort, disillusionment, and desperation are often rooted in an estrangement from God and from not having that faithful intimacy, which has a strength greater than the concrete foundation of the World Trade Center or the anchoring of the countless bridges over which hundreds of thousands travel daily. The strength of faithful intimacy girds our bridge over troubled waters and helps our faith stand firm when the storms of life rage. Anchored in that faith of faithful intimacy, we come to know a joy and peace incomprehensible. As one holds fast to this faith of faithful intimacy we are open to our own magnificence, to that of others, and are able to garner the courage to change where warranted. Often low self-esteem and low self-worth cause persons to project their insecurities on others, leading to dysfunctional behavior. When a dysfunctional leader of an institution or a family craves power and recognition more than he or she craves to be well and healed, we end up with sick institutions and sick families. Balance and wellness requires that everyone emerge from the fog of denial, name the culprit, and then create a plan of action to embark on a road toward change. The result of embracing change is for everyone to become well. Whatever impedes our total health impedes our relationship with God. Our bodies are temples. Our communities are networks of sacred spaces.

Meditation 3

In late afternoon,
When dreariness descends,

We need only remember,
The blessedness of life:
We breathe; we have hope,
We are loved by God.

Most of us can choose
To live fully, creatively, magnificently.
Yet some are trapped.
Those graced with health can choose
Relational oneness or victimhood:
Perfected, fractured numbness.

Each moment we choose again.
Time need not cheat us;
Illness and pain
Need not cripple
Our spontaneity, our joy.

As integrated body, mind, spirit,
We balance moments of ecstasy and futility,
Knowing always
In some sector of the totality of us:
God cares, hope abides,
We are not our problems.

We have a choice:
We can start over right now,
And right now, and now,
Even if that now,
Must wait until tomorrow.

Even the most joyous and balanced person will have a "bad hair day"—a day when things tend to fall apart despite one's faith, planning, or expertise. The curious thing is that many times when we sense things are falling apart things are actually falling together. Sometimes we have to let things "fall apart" to get well. If we are living with unmanageable debt, then we need to let go of that expensive lifestyle to be financially healthy. If we are employed in a job that is beyond our capabilities and imagination, then for mental and emotional health we need to find a job more suited to our persona and our talents. If we are in a relationship that is lethal, harmful, or physically, psychologically, or emotionally abusive, then we need to break that connection. Unfortunately, most people trapped by destructive living cannot see what has transpired: classic denial.

Denial is deadly. So many times all the signs indicate that somebody is in trouble and needs help. If we fail to listen, see, and offer ministry we may end up with a deep tragedy. Many persons who have addictions never get well because they cannot admit that they have a problem or that there may be a hopeful solution or that there may be hope. Persons who commit suicide often scream out, begging for help, but friends and family sometimes fail to hear, and when they do, it is often too late. We need to be attentive to the feelings and concerns of family, friends, and neighbors. Does this mean that we have to live their lives for them or be at their beck and call? No; but it does mean that we can do appropriate referral, we can lift up people in prayer, and we can listen when needed. Dysfunctional behavior needs to cease. When we really understand that human beings are created in God's image, and when we live out this context, we are able to identify inappropriate behavior and take steps to turn toward healthy options. The church and other religious institutions must be the ears of tolerance and the voices of hope.

The freedom that comes with a balanced life of positive self-esteem and self-worth is priceless. Conversely, when we are not in tune or when we are trapped in inadequacy, we generate a culture of victims and entitlement and scenarios of compound hurt. Intensified, exponential hurt can result in fractured numbness or explode into a catastrophe. The concept of the integrated self is a model that can embrace health, healing, and people living with difference, integrity, ambiguity, and certainty. God created us as a palette of dynamic energy with many colors of thought, being, and presence. We are given opportunities to be stretched, to celebrate, and to grow. Not all of us can do, or need to do, the same tasks in life. Can you imagine a world without artists or truck drivers, surgeons or gardeners, teachers or garbage collectors? What if all of us had the same skin color, same hair color, same body types, same interests, or the same aspirations? How boring and mundane! Differences mean we have choices. Not all choices are easy to make, particularly as we begin to age and we can no longer do all the things "we used to do." Nevertheless, as we gain self-knowledge and gain a greater appreciation for how difficult, yet how fulfilling, a healthy, balanced, integrated sense of body, mind, and spirit can be, we can live lovingly in the moment.

Meditation 4

Tightropes strung across the poles,
Acrobats walking across,
Like us when we make decisions
From the bowels of fear and degradation.

Choosing to beat ourselves up,
We forget that the One
Who affords the creativity
To string the tightrope,
Is the One who created us,
Who lives within and around us.
What a relief to know we're not all alone.

In that moment of being,
When we know we are not alone—
We sense that sweet revelation of
Oneness with the universe, with God,
Such oneness brings serenity,
Balance, joyous in itself;
And health, as we release the weight
Of having to do, know, be, and understand all.

The gift of laughter is crucial to our well-being. Laughing creates a buffer where we can relax and not take ourselves too seriously. Laughing helps to release pent-up emotions. Sometimes we laugh at inappropriate times out of embarrassment. Sometimes we laugh when we are nervous or taken by surprise. Laughter ought to be an expression of joy and never the tool of ridicule. We are often so fragile that we are like tightrope walkers without the skill to maintain balance in the gymnastics of life. When we become wound too tightly we often operate from fear. Fear in itself is not bad. Fear that stifles our creativity and smothers our joy can be deadly. Sometimes we rely on fear when we do not have a handle on failure or when we are intimidated by success. Even so, that fear is just a feeling and it need not inhibit our health. When we face fear head-on (see chapter 2) we can move on.

Sometimes we use fear to validate our insecurities. We become so self-absorbed over what we perceive as our weaknesses that we cannot hear the melodies of strength or of new possibilities within ourselves. When we successfully embrace these insecurities we become masters of self-critique, self-flagellation: we beat ourselves up so thoroughly in the hope that no one else will do so. What if we can excel, then what? What if God really does love us and will forgive us? We can tell God things we might not tell another living soul. God is our biggest cheerleader and confidante. God wants us to do well and bask in divine glory. God wants us to be good stewards and respectful of the gifts God has given us. We come from a living God, a God who lives in us. Awareness of this divine, incarnated, blessedness within brings serenity and harmony, balanced joy and prayerful hope toward new possibility, and the freedom to live as an integrated whole in a community with others and at peace.

Responsive Readings

Responsive Reading 1

Leader: We give thanks for seasons and time and the opportunities to find balance in our lives.

People: **As Ecclesiastes people, we celebrate the time to plant and harvest the fruit of our thoughts and deeds. We honor our ancestors and their contributions to our family and society.**

Leader: We give thanks for the birth of babies and new ideas; we know that some things must change and others must die. We bow to Divine wisdom and efficiency in all things.

People: **As Ecclesiastes people, we celebrate the times of breaking down and building up; we honor diversity in our communities, our thinking, and in the way we worship God.**

Leader: For this day, which brings decision making, waiting, growing, and sharing love, we appreciate God and how God blesses the work of liberation and social justice.

People: **As Ecclesiastes people, we give witness to the times when we weep and laugh, mourn and dance.**

Leader: For a time to celebrate the Sabbath, for quiet moments, for discernment, for speaking, listening, and silence, we rejoice.

All: **As Ecclesiastes people, we recognize the times to be, as we seek the righteousness of God.**

One of life's gifts to us is the ability to share appreciation. Some people are so wounded that they think to say "thank you" is to show weakness. Offering thanks creates an open dialogue with God and with humanity. Thanks never minimizes, but reflects openness, awareness, and value. Consciousness about value presses us to live an ethical life where our behavior grows out of our sense of the sacred. Witnessing to the sacred involves our worship, prayers, and spiritual disciplines, and honors our individual and collective past. Honoring the past helps us see the present without needing to know what will transpire in the future.

Some people do not need enemies because they are their own worst nightmare. They are self-destructive and self-deprecating, denying their own God-given magnificence. When one finally experiences the Divine within, it is the beginning of true relationship and of being open to change and liberation. With such freedom comes the desire to worship daily in every aspect of our lives, not out of coercion, but out of joy.

Responsive Reading 2

Leader: In a world of many ideas and cultures, many peoples and ways of being, we honor the wisdom that lies beneath all that is good and blessed.

People: **In the quest of holiness we salute all that is sacred and all that takes time to be aware of God's presence.**

Leader: In a world of many songs and prayers, of many flowers and trees, we celebrate the many beings in our world who support us, providing food, medicines, beauty, and oxygen.

People: **In the quest of holiness we honor the Holy One as we honor the gifts of time and labor and of accomplishments making a difference.**

Leader: We sing the songs of life, we see the artistry in all designs and nature, we scale the crests of difficulty, we sit quietly at the plateaus of sorrow.

People: **In the quest of holiness we give ourselves permission to make mistakes and experience grace in the process.**

Leader: In a world of laughter and tears, of many languages and dialects, we honor all healthy modes of communication for renewal and blessing.

All: **In the quest of holiness we yearn for justice and mercy; we yearn for the lessening of violence and for the wellness of all people, especially our children; we desire the cessation of war and the concerted effort for peace.**

Given the power and diversity within God it makes sense that human beings can be so alike yet so different. The differences become a variation on a theme, as people are different but their basic physiology and the experiences necessary for survival are the same worldwide. Together the differences are the movements and motifs of a symphony: many instruments, many performers, and yet one huge musical work. We must deal with dissonance and consonance, rhythm or pulses, tempo or time, slow or fast. Different individuals move to different drummers; others want the safety of the old hymns and standard classical repertoire. Some want to dance to country, some to R & B, others to rap, yet others to waltzes. Nevertheless, on some level, we all want to dance. In health, we embrace the music and move and feel good. In feeling good, we know holiness. In knowing holiness, we honor God, ourselves, and life itself: we know peace.

Responsive Reading 3

Leader: Lift up your voices and sing of the glory of God, of early dawn and evening sunsets, when we see the resplendent Divine in the colors in the sky.

People: **We applaud the gift of serenity that comes with acceptance as we make life decisions that work for ourselves and our families, living out God's call on our lives.**

Leader: Lift up your pens and pencils and write out words of praise and thanksgiving for all blessings.

People: **We applaud the gift of serenity as we grow in grace and love, to serve God and to honor the community about us.**

Leader: Lift up your thoughts and think about the beauty and simplicity of diversity and the opportunity we have to love one another.

People: **We applaud the gift of serenity as we see the many places where peace is the norm, and focus less on the domination of violence.**

Leader: Lift up your arms in prayer to God, to honor every gift, every person that has made a difference, every child who has not gone astray.

All: **We applaud the gift of serenity as we learn to speak, act, and live in love.**

Lifting is a dynamic act that implies upward motion, improvement, and accomplishments. In lifting, in raising our voices, our bodies, and our spirits in praise, we come closer to God and closer to fully embodying the love of God. Lifting and blessing God is an act of giving and receiving: we give praise to God, God gives love and well-being to us. Because of God's generosity, we experience the seasons, the sacred, and serenity—the gift of clarity and quiet, where the storms of life may rage but where we are able to stand and be affirmed. To know serenity is the gift of peace, security, mutuality, and sacred silence. Serenity affords one freedom from agitation, violence, and turmoil: a sense of calm. To be calm amid deadlines, stress, ambiguity, and times of change is a blessing. Such blessedness is part of the threads that hold our integrated selves together in unity. Such blessedness penetrates our daily lives if we are open to seeing and experiencing this sacredness. Then we cannot embrace denial, disrespect, or anxiety. The power of this blessedness allows us to be affirming of the elegance and simplicity of diversity and the opportunity we have to love one another. Loving one another becomes something that is special and that we cannot live without.

Responsive Reading 4

Leader: At the end of the day, at noon, and at daybreak, we know God is with us, God cares for us: this is our heritage and the source of our strength.

People: **Each moment of the day, God cares for us. We rejoice in the truth of this claim; we bless God.**

Leader: As the dew sparkles on the petals of roses, as water falls from melted snow from mountains, as butterflies emerge from cocoons, we know God is in each dimension of the universe.

People: **We sing songs of thanksgiving and pray for the wisdom and courage to follow God's leading in our lives.**

Leader: We pause in awe at the grandeur of divine work, in gratitude that we too are part of God's world.

People: **Each moment of the day, we can stop and pray for the renewal of all life, for better human stewardship, for collaboration toward making our world a place of justice and mercy.**

Leader: As afternoon becomes evening, we can say, "Thank You, God!" for giving us another beautiful day where we had a chance to touch someone's life with a message of love and hope.

All: **Each moment of the day, at the most ordinary times, we can celebrate the love God has for us: how blessed we are! Hallelujah!**

Some people do not know God in a way that is meaningful in their lives. They may recognize good and beauty but are not familiar with the author of that good and that splendor. Some people claim to know God but are so mean-spirited, so hurtful, or so oppressive that it quickly becomes apparent that their concept of God is skewed, warped, and harmful. When one experiences God that unique relationship creates a format for knowing perfect peace. This peace does not ultimately depend on how one feels or what is going on in one's life. The peace of God is exquisite and delightful; it gives one a sense of extraordinary calm amid confusion and ill will. This peace does not make one complacent, jaded, or insensitive to one's surroundings. This peace allows one to come from a place of tranquility where one can give others, in a nonjudgmental way, the room to be themselves. This peace allows one the room to be who God created him or her to be, and moves one to make a difference. This peace moves us to be ecologically sensitive and to shift from a mind-set of domination to one of appreciation and responsible stewardship.

Prayers of Commitment

Prayer of Commitment 1

We embrace our lives, ourselves—spirit, body, mind—as one, to be in community with others as we honor God and the gift of life.

We release the pain of hopelessness, of being fractured and broken. Help us know the depths and desires of our heart toward joy. Help us own up to the things we do not like about ourselves so that we can accept those things we cannot change. Help us realize destructive habits so that we can change them and honor our whole selves as sacred. Grant us the insight to see the differences between those things and habits in our lives that serve us well and those experiences that cause harm to ourselves and others. May we take courage to live life in a totally healthy manner. May we have the staying power to stay the course when it seems that our progress is too slow. Help us take small steps on a daily basis so that we may go the distance toward wholeness and being healthy. Help us remove ourselves from environments where people seek to hurt us. Deliver us from needing to make life difficult for ourselves when an easier, gentler path is available. Help us love ourselves and you so much, O God, as prayerful acts of worship.

When life becomes overwhelming we can revisit the place where we can know love—in the presence of God. God created us to be one in body, mind, and spirit; to be whole, integrated persons. Because there are so many pulls on our lives, a sense of being integrated may be difficult. Of course it is much easier to say "Live an integrated life and be a whole person" than it is to daily live this way. Although accomplishing this level of integration sounds simple, it may not be easy to maintain. The complexity or ease of embracing one's total health as a way of life will depend upon one's lifestyle and one's priorities.

Working twenty hour days does not make for ease in maintaining serenity. Eating junk food and becoming a couch potato does little to stimulate balance and health. Perhaps in examining one's goals and options it will become clear that a more disciplined life will reap a greater sense of clarity and purpose. With courage and the support of others what appear as mountains may actually become speed bumps, and then become molehills before our very eyes. If one can only make a small step forward, then many small steps together become big steps. Making changes toward a more healthy sense of self and life is pleasing to God and gives us a better quality of life.

Prayer of Commitment 2

We celebrate the beauty of knowing God and knowing ourselves as children of God in faith, hope, and justice. We acknowledge our need to love and be loved, and vow to listen carefully as part of our ministry to ourselves. We give thanks for the children who remind us that life is marvelous and that we can try to do things that feel impossible. We are grateful that children remind us that it is all right to cry and that they remind us of the importance of being nurtured and of nurturing others.

We give thanks for the tediousness of life that causes us to stop and think and assess who we are, why we do what we do, and what needs to change in the context of historical memory. We have a great sense of gratitude for adolescents and teens, who remind us that life is full of promise yet difficult and often confusing. We salute adults who work to make our world a better place, and who also make mistakes.

We honor our senior adults who have come to the season of sunset and eventide as they teach us lessons they have learned well. We ask for peace for all who struggle with who they are and what they are to do in this world to make a difference. May God grant us all the ability to listen to each other well, to empathize, to ask for excellence, and to accept each of us where we are.

The days we forget to celebrate God and ourselves are the days we miss something special. To celebrate God and humanity is to worship, to praise—in formal and informal settings—and is an act of love. As human beings, we need to love and we need to be loved out of covenant reciprocation. God calls us to love with reciprocity and mutuality through a faithful covenant commitment to be in relationship with others. We can love with integrity if we listen to the call of God, to our own needs, and to the needs of others. Each time we have an opportunity to love another human being in a respectful, appreciative manner reconnects us with God.

God is a loving presence with us in many ways, particularly in the presence of other human beings. This love never demeans, oppresses, or needs to control. Love, a spiritual gift of freedom, is foundational for well-being and for creating new, healthy ways of being. Love undergirds thanksgiving, faith, and hope. Love bolsters peace and brings joy. Love shapes our listening when we care and want to make a difference.

Prayer of Commitment 3

On those days when life seems too difficult to contemplate, when we are so confused that we do not know which end is up, we pray, Gracious Spirit, that You will send angels to show us the way and to let us know that our lives matter. In the bounty of Your creation sometimes we feel lost and unimportant, that no matter what we do, we never do enough; that nobody really cares about how we feel and what we need. There are moments when our lives make no sense to us and we struggle to keep our heads above water. There are times when we make mistakes that cause great harm to ourselves and others, when we knew better. Majestic God, help us be gentle with ourselves in these moments and pull us closer to You that we might be on the path of righteousness. We give thanks for Your goodness and Your mercy.

Even when we have a grave sense of loss and when we are depressed, lonely, or angry, we need to know Your love. We need to know that You care and that someone bearing Your light also cares. Help us see the caring, loving spaces in our lives. Help us have a sense of balance, to know when to stop and when to go; when to work and when to rest; when to shout out and when to be silent. We desire peace and Your presence. Be with us in our quest for Your holiness.

The stories of humanity throughout the world show that difficulties, confusion, and pain exist amid and alongside God's glory. Sometimes we feel horribly alone at these moments, even when among family or in a room full of friends. Some days we need more compassion and nurturing; other days we need more space and solitude. One key factor for living a healthy life on the continuum between needing attention and needing quiet is being able to ask for what we want. Some of us think that because we are called by God to serve that we must be doormats. Some of us think that the world revolves around us and thus people need to wait on us, without a sense of reciprocity or fairness. Either extreme becomes problematic when on a quest for an integrated self.

Arrogance, narcissism, false modesty, and misplaced pride are not helpful attitudes. They are ways of being alone and without community. At those moments, we often need a kind voice to say, "Peace, be still." A life steeped in peace and serenity would be able to see the fallacies of arrogance, narcissism, and false modesty or misplaced pride. A life steeped in peace and serenity would provide a means for becoming more secure and comfortable with the self. Clarity about an individual's gifts and obstacles provide a healthy context for being true to oneself and for recognizing the areas of growth.

Prayer of Commitment 4

Joyful, joyful are the moments when we stop and listen for Your voice, O Loving God. You have walked with us, You have talked with us, and You have carried us over infinite horizons of seconds, minutes, and hours in our lives. We praise You for your willingness to be with us. We thank You for giving us loved ones who have been Your loving witnesses to us. Help us take time to listen well for the good news. Help us take time to listen to the pain and hurt of ourselves and others, in a thoughtful way, where we may help prevent irrevocable harm and danger. Help us take time to be holy, to rest, to nurture ourselves toward a balanced life as we honor the gift of life.

Help us love in meaningful ways. Help us love our children and teach us how to parent, that we may help break the cycle of woundedness and lifelong pain that results from being brought up by parents who do not know how to love, affirm, care for, or discipline children in healthy ways. Help us be the village that not only raises our children, but a village who nurtures and provides room and support for adults whose lives need transformation.

Listening well is an art and a science. To listen for God requires a sensitivity of ongoing insight, to note how to talk to God and how to respond when God answers. God has promised to never forsake us, and that is good news. In this vein, God is Immanuel, with us, loving us, protecting us, and sending messengers to bear glad tidings of good news. The good news is that God loves us and that we can experience salvation—liberation from anxiety and oppression. We are called to be liberated and to help liberate others. One of the tasks of community is to share this wonderful message and to be a vehicle and catalyst for change. To be situated in such a moving, powerful role requires integrity, peace, communication, love, sincere confession, and forgiveness. Without integrity the trust factor between various people cannot be initiated or maintained. Peace is one fruit of the love that flows throughout and provides serenity and a gift of quiet sacredness. In prayer, in the asking and listening, we can confess the pain and confusion. After this acknowledgment and clarity one can then entertain the process of forgiveness. We need to forgive injuries done to us. But the forgiveness and healing cannot start until we say something went wrong. And, although some acts of violence are deeply irresponsible and reprehensible, to live in covenant faith with holistic health, balance, and serenity, we must ultimately release and when appropriate for us, forgive, though we never forget.

Chapter 7

Spirituality: Looking for a Way Out

The impulse of life,
The entry toward death,
Combine pain and passion.
Beginnings and endings,
The parentheses bracketing.
The breaths and beats
Of soulful community.

Rushing, running, hustling,
Moving hither, thither, yon.
Lives too full,
Time too short;
Not stuck in yesterday,
Not obsessing about tomorrow:
Time to live and love and listen.

Listen for your heart,
Your soul, your mind,
That's crying out for some quiet time.
Phew! Time to stop running
Away from yourself,
Time to be still and know,
We are all made in God's image,
Yet, we are not God.

Isn't that good news?

Life has so many faces: expressions of delight and disdain, elegance and errors. Sometimes we get trapped into focusing on outer appearances, external trappings, and acquired goods as indicators of beauty, status, and self-esteem. Things make us comfortable but ultimately do not make us happy. Part of having a balanced life, wherein one easily experiences the sacred in new ways, is to look for inner beauty and strength. One can also set priorities and focus on those goals that lead one to experiencing life as ministry. Life has many faces, with many colors, sizes, and shapes. Such shadings, from the palest ivory to the deepest ebony, are the colors in God's palette of humanity. The colors depict God's covenantal joy and imagination: the impulse that sparks life itself. In our comings and goings we celebrate the divine impulse within us: when blood flows and air circulates, and when we laugh, cry, speak, sing, and make love. When we honor that divine impulse we realize there is enough time to do what we need to do: to empower our individual and communal ministries. We are also willing to embrace the divine in new ways, which allow us to be responsible, to transcend, and to be transformed.

Meditations

Meditation 1

Looking and listening,
We experience the sacred:
Lurking over the moments
Of lost and found,
In our musings.
Just a breeze
Signals our appreciation of the day.

New ways of looking and listening,
New possibilities, new relationships.
New thoughts,
Shifting stereotypes
To the attics of our minds,
To the cellars of our hearts,
Welcome all, to the living rooms of our spirits.

We wash our weary eyes,
With the spirit of God.
Releasing the tears of yesterday,
The angst of tomorrow.
For the first time,

Being in today, and seeing,
Who we are.

Starting with Genesis 1 and ending with the prologue of the Gospel of John (John 1:1-18) as the bookends to guide our biblical safari, we sense the awesomeness of the Spirit of God. "In the beginning, God" is pronouncement and proclamation. The Hebrew term for spirit, *rûah*, also means wind or air in motion, breath, mind. *Rûah* moves over the face of the deep and creation begins. In Genesis and in John, creation through spoken and symbolic word provides a catalyst for new life. Spirited words and expressions generate a heightened sense of the sacred. Spirit is life-giving, producing vitality, ability, intelligence, and divine connectedness (Gen. 1:2; Exod. 31:3; Gen. 41:38). Amid this spirit one can know vulnerability and brokenness (Gen. 45:27; Exod. 6:9); jealousy and wisdom (Num. 5:13, 30; Deut. 34:9); be willful (Exod. 31:21); be faithful and hasty (Prov. 11:13; 14:29); and be wounded or know excellence (Prov. 18:14; 17:27).

The character of the spirit, *rûah*, is multifaceted, including judgment with understanding (Isa. 4:4; 11:2); and grief (Isa. 54:6). *Rûah* signals movement, for example: being poured upon (Isa. 32:5); and being taken up (Isa. 11:24). *Rûah's* other emotional factors include being new (Exod. 18:31); being troubled (Dan. 2:3); and being stirred up (Hag. 1:14). *Rûah*, the spirit, creates power (Mic. 3:8) and can connote its antonym: the Queen of Sheba has no more *rûah* or breath, she was so overwhelmed or breathless. *Rûah*, the spirit, makes one full of grace, holiness, and excellence (Zech. 12:10; Dan. 4:8, 6:3, 5:2). *Rûah* pertains to that which is distinctive about human life— the spiritual— that we are created in God's image, *Imago Dei*, implying the immaterial consciousness of humanity. *Rûah*, the spirit, pertains to angelic, supernatural messengers sent by God (1 Sam. 16:23), or to God's spiritual personality (Isa. 31:3). God's spirit engages in redemption through regeneration, creation, or empowering of a coming messiah (Ezek. 36:26-27; Job 26:13; Isa. 42:1, 62:1).[1]

In the New Testament, *pneuma* denotes air, breath, rational soul, vital principle, and Holy Spirit (e.g., life, spirit, mind, and ghost). The nature and function of *pneuma* varies. Some spirits are unclean, poor, or strong (Matt. 12:43, 5:3; Luke 1:80). Some spirits are of God, doing the work of God in truth, salvation, quickening, and faith (Matt. 3:6; John 15:26; 1 Cor. 5:5, 15:45; 2 Cor. 4:13). Some spirits give forth messages, engage in rejoicing, are meek, foster unity, and nurture renewal (Luke 10:21; 1 Cor. 4:21; Eph. 4:3, 4:23). *Pneuma,* the spirit, also affords humanity the possibility of engaging in particular practices for the sake of spiritual discipline and survival, as one prays in the spirit (1 Cor. 14:15; Eph. 6:18); stands fast in the spirit (Phil. 1:27); and embraces the sword of the spirit (Eph. 6:17). The spirit also brings forth glory and enables one to confess (1 Pet. 4:14; 1 John 4:3).

In Matthew and Mark, the Spirit of God is given to humanity to transcend human weakness or the demonic. The Spirit, used anthropologically, is the place of feelings and perceptions, and is God's power to do special acts. A community may be blessed in the past and the present by the prophetic Spirit. The Holy Spirit, often referred to as the *Holy Ghost,* is God's extraordinary power, beyond human capability, usually in a context that references Christ. In Luke and Acts, the Spirit is God's creative, life-giving power, which Christ gives out to the community after the Resurrection (Luke 24:49; Acts 2:33). Whereas believers only have the Spirit through Jesus Christ, the Spirit can become manifest outwardly as at Pentecost and manifests in those inspired witnesses of Jesus Christ. Healing comes through faith in Jesus, in the name of Jesus, through prayer, in contact with disciples, and with Jesus' power itself. All baptized persons possess the Spirit, which endows the believer with the heightened gift of faith.

Paul writes in a backdrop of Greek and Judaic influence about the Spirit. For Paul, *pneuma* is the exalted Christ. Union with this exalted Christ guarantees believers a spiritual life set in the community. Paul sees the crucifixion and the resurrection as the crucial period; one receives the spiritual body as a gift of God to be given in this resurrection. In waiting for the return of Christ with believer's resurrection, the Spirit's existence indicates what will come. In addition, Paul sees *pneuma* as the power of faith *(pistis),* the antithesis of flesh, as the mode of intercession, of prayer before God and one's neighbor, and the gift and power of the *eschaton*, traditionally that sense of end times or last days. Many contemporary theologians refer to the *eschaton* as goal orientation, understanding that what one expects to happen at death is clear by how one lives life in the present; a sense of lived salvific experience.

For John, Spirit does not manifest in the same way as in the Lucan texts. John sees the encounter with the Creator (Parent/Father) in the Son. The Paraclete, the Spirit of Truth, represents reality as opposed to appearance. Like Jesus, the Paraclete teaches, witnesses, and preaches about sin. The Spirit is alongside Jesus and Jesus comes in the Paraclete, but they are not identical. *Pneuma* is the power of Jesus' preaching as redeemer, wherein the divine encounters the human. For Ephesians, *pneuma* pertains to the power within the community's growth. In the Pastoral Epistles, the work of the Spirit relates to the new birth that places humanity in hope and justification. In Hebrews, the meaning of Spirit is complex. The Spirit speaks through scripture (3:7, 9:8), works in miracles (2:4, 6:4), and signals God's eschatological grace (10:29). In 1 Peter, *pneuma* is generally concerned with powers of sanctification. In 2 Peter, the Spirit inspires the accepted canonical scripture. In Revelation, *pneuma*, given by a demon or God, is an essential source with a key focus on the Spirit of prophecy (Rev. 19:10). The Spirit, the exalted Lord, speaks to the community.

Meditation 2

Many bodies, many spirits, many minds
Connecting, weaving, moving—
Creating tapestries of divine threads,
Woven majestically, patterns strong.
Love mixed with hate,
Surrounded by mystery,
Boredom tempered by discovery,
Jaded by reality.

Spiritual life,
Weaving a oneness of regal self,

Luxuriant in the beautiful symmetry,
Of divine gossamer.
Ever holding,
Not infringing
Upon one's freedom to be or
Embroidered with divine fitness.

Ah! The wisdom of the ages
Hangs resplendent with
Clouds of witnesses,
Doing the work of prayer.
Sustaining, holding, covering us:
A rainbow of believers.

Daily life has many kinds of energy, particularly within humanity as bodies and as minds and as spirits: short, medium, tall; sluggish, moderate, brilliant; loving, soulful, or hateful. So connected, we see the beauty of community or we choose to be disruptive, divided over human categories through ignorance and hate. Sometimes living oppression comes from fear: fear colors racism, sexism, class or elitism, homophobia, ageism, and prejudice against those who are physically and mentally challenged. The many colors and sizes and life experiences of people form the tapestries of God's created humanity. If we are open to seeing the mysteries that unfold among peoples of the world, we will not be bored and we will have marvelous discoveries. In the discoveries of others we learn more about ourselves. We can become parts of other tapestries and can transcend fear when we seek God's wisdom, efficiency, and peace. As we have peace with ourselves and God, we can be at peace with others. We can identify when others have genuine problems or when we are projecting our own fears onto others or when others project their fears onto us. Sometimes we need quiet to begin to see just how much alike we are.

When we listen carefully and remain in present time with others, whether they are similar to us or unlike us, we can begin to embrace the fullness of our spiritual lives. The fullness of our spiritual selves expands when we connect with other souls, where under the inspiration of the Holy Spirit a tapestry unfolds that depicts the weaving together of many communities into a resplendent unity. Why is it that most people think babies are beautiful, are cute regardless of race, but somehow as those infants become children and adults all of a sudden "those people" become problematic? A spiritual life presses us to acknowledge differences and live with them, free from ignorance or fear. Such freedom presses us to be noble, elegant, and just.

Freedom is being solitary among many and being comfortable with that oneness. Freedom is being many among many and not demonizing those who make up a community of one. Since God has no hands but our hands and no eyes but our eyes it behooves us to use these hands to effect the freedom of all. To appreciate similarities and differences fully is to experience the wisdom of the ages. To prepare ourselves for the blessing of this wisdom is an exercise steeped in faith and surrounded by prayer. Prayer, a ritual of preparation so that we might be ready to know ourselves and others well, changes things. The more open we are to others, the more open we are to ourselves. Prayer interconnects ourselves, and prayer gives us time to have conversation with God amid moments of reflection. A vital prayer life is critical to possessing the ability to explore new, positive options of being an individual and of being in community.

Meditation 3

Spirit, wind, blowing, blowing, blowing,
Sending forth old ways of being,
Bringing out new ways of thinking, being, doing.
Spirit, strong, joyful song,
For the first days ever that we meet.

Releasing old ways—
Of needing to control everyone and everything.
Truly experiencing divine Grace;
Reveling in sweet surrender;
Nonsacrificial in tone;
Often uncomfortable in depth;
Blessed in reality.

Championing new types of listening,
Walking through the moors of mental minefields;
Poised to destroy and be destroyed.
Moving toward contemplation,
Deep thoughts about the options
Needed for the salvation and the survival of all.

The waking existence of most human beings involves times when we act, think, or engage in a state of being. Like the spirit and wind, acting involves movement, accomplishments, and deeds completed, performed, and simulated. Some acts occur with grace and integrity; others violate ethics and customs yet are legally justified. Other acts are positively wrong, bad, and evil. There are good, bad, indifferent, and ambiguous spirits. When embracing new models of community and of humanity it is imperative that we remain open to the movement of the Spirit in all decision making and strategizing. Activating new models does not deny or denigrate previous history. Clarity and practical changes require that institutional history be available. History serves as a contextual apparatus that helps us discern what has been attempted, what worked, and what did not work. Listening well is an effort to avoid putting old wine into new wine skins, to avoid taking a flight of fancy about requirements to affect transformation, to lessen the tendency toward false expectations, and to the minimizing of the value that such work can make.

Clarification about recent history also provides a forum for releasing old habits, particularly the need to control or the compulsion to be controlled. Either stance is problematic. The need to control eradicates mutuality. The need to be controlled removes freedom. By faith one can surrender self-destructive behavior to God. Surrender and sacrifice are not synonymous here. Surrender means to release, to yield to the control, power, or possession of another through invitation, demand, or coercion; to give up completely or to agree to forgo something. Sacrifice often connotes an offering to a deity; to kill a victim on an altar; a destruction or surrender of something for the sake of something else. A new spiritual life calls for surrender and for listening.

The manner in which we listen and what tempers our hearing are important. When one is self-assured and cares about meaningful dialogue and hopeful solutions, intelligent conversations can ensue where all parties learn, grow, and are willing to make the necessary changes for the good of each and the good of all. When coming from uncertainty, jealousy, misunderstandings, or incorrect information and bias, open dialogue is impossible. Wounded spirits and the projection of personal ills on others tend to be the norm. When persons are willing to grow and face the demons arising from their past hurts, from the legacies of oppression and injustice, together with feelings of insecurity and inadequacy, then, and only then, does the process of healing begin. Families and communities can come together to wrestle with their issues and their dysfunctional lives, because they are able to look for and see the *sacred in each other*. In looking for the sacred in each other we are better able to see differences, with flexibility and tolerance, without needing to erase or suppress the differences, so that we agree to disagree and learn the art of compromise.

Meditation 4

Mistakes, ambiguities, misunderstandings,
Cloud our realities,
Causing wounded spirits, hurt feelings,
Broken dreams and relationships,
Living with ourselves and in community,
Rising above the mundane,
Looking for the sacred.

Fairness and ease
Sometimes reign supreme, though rarely.
Daily, we meet the bumps,
Obstacles large and small.
Bending and stretching our realities.
With the desire for salvation
Comes the willingness
Not to hermitage, but for a blessed life.

143

O joyous moment,
The freedom of salvation.
A cornucopia of bountiful peace,
Making way for transformation:
"Confess and name the past;
Repent and offer blessings;
Reveling in the holiness of justice."

Some days we take all that is around us for granted and never realize the work, the time, the planning, and the prayer that characterize the foundations of all that we see. To complain and find fault is easy. To stand and appreciate what is, without a jaded sensibility, is difficult. Before we can earnestly and hopefully see the sacred in ourselves, in one another, and in the world, we must be willing to take a close, authentic look. Even then, we will see from the context of our own lives, biases, and dreams. When we prayerfully and carefully look, we may see the beauty, the ordinariness, or the ugliness of the situation. We may sense the passion or vision that fueled a movement. We may see the glazed-over eyes whose dreams have died. We know the eager anticipation of those yet daring and youthful enough to hold fast to their dreams. In absorbing all this information we become vulnerable to the revelations of the pain and the possibilities of others. If we want to engage in collaborative work such revelations are opportunities for us to bond toward truly being a neighbor.

Together as neighbors we can make a difference and develop an ethos and ethic of fairness. Some neighbors are so wounded that they have no idea of the possibilities of living a life of justice and solidarity: everyone is out to get them, no one cares, and they are dispensable. Much systemic oppression makes the experience of being hunted real for many in our society, especially the poor. In the United States, racism has been named as a reason though many pretend that we no longer have a race problem. The level to which we deny classism and elitism is nothing short of amazing. We deny the realities of class and fail to address our economic system of exploitative capitalism and ruthless mercantilism. We blind our eyes to struggles and obstacles of class, gender, race, and sexual orientation, which make the lives of many unmanageable and difficult. A quest for holiness provides a different avenue or approach to life. On the streets of tranquility and peace, one can build communities based on collaboration, mutuality, respect, and love. On the streets of blessing and love, one can build societies of justice and reconciliation. On the streets of salvation and hope, one can build communities of salvation and wholeness.

Responsive Readings

Responsive Reading 1

Leader: Open up our hearts that we may know ourselves as part of a loving community called by Divine invitation to embrace peace, unity, and charity.

People: **In peace and unity we come to serve and love one another so that violence will be reduced as justice spreads across our land like a cool breeze.**

Leader: We rejoice in knowing that we are made of God and that we can be healed and know our true selves; stripped of lies, false pride, and mean-spiritedness.

People: **We surrender to God, that the light of God might shine brightly within us—radiating; drawing others to the gospel of love and responsibility.**

Leader: We honor the different colors of the rainbow—alive and well in the many hues and tones of humanity, our differences and our similarities; respecting all.

People: **In peace and unity we bless God's people as people who love and are loved; we pray for our well-being, faith, strength, and total salvation.**

Leader: We accept the challenges to be better neighbors and to release the need to manipulate others for greed, fame, power, and self-aggrandizement.

All: In peace and unity we welcome inclusive ways of being with those who think, look, act, and worship in ways different from us. Praise to God who created us all.

The possibilities, which we can imagine, reflect our vision of God. If we embrace a punishing, vindictive God, we make excuses for all the pain and evil that occur in our lives. If we have a benevolent, merciful, and just God, we focus on possibilities, allowing room for mysteries and the unexplainable. We also know that the inexcusable is often the result of human frailty and wrongdoing. If we accept that God is love and that we are created in God's image, our norm for existence will grow out of loving blessedness. If we recognize our gifts and our priorities, and we pray for the courage to do that which we can, we will be miracle workers. In a context of loving blessedness we celebrate the varieties of spiritual gifts, the varieties of persons, and the varieties of experiences. We can confess our shortcomings and find ways to break the patterns of destructive behavior. When loving blessedness is the context for our life's goals, we are empowered to be more inclusive of others, to appreciate that God can choose to self-reveal in a variety of ways, and to learn to live together celebrating our differences and similarities in peace.

Responsive Reading 2

Leader: We celebrate our religious and family traditions when we look for new ways of engaging in formal and daily worship as we glimpse the sacred.

People: **In living a sacred life we honor the extraordinary and ordinary ways in which we know the daily presence and reality of God.**

Leader: We listen for the voice of God in the Bible, in other written texts, and in the stories of people, God's messengers on earth.

People: **In living a sacred life we wait patiently for God to fix our hearts as we pledge to be good stewards of our talents and our time.**

Leader: We see life as a miraculous adventure, where we are privy to know a special divine relationship with others, in covenant with us and God.

People: **We reject the need to practice any oppression based on race, creed, color, gender, sexual orientation, age, economic status, or public persona.**

Leader: We acknowledge that in every moment we are called to be a disciple, a teacher, and a friend, sharing the joy of God's bounty and goodness.

All: **In living a sacred life we take the time to be holy, to laugh, to play, and to rest; knowing the importance of celebrating the Sabbath daily, of seeking sacred silences.**

Much of our lives are involved in rituals. Religious and family celebrations can be powerful moments of sharing and affirmation. From daily prayer on arising, retiring, and at meals, and singing psalms and anthems together, to weekly worship, baptisms, weddings, anniversaries, reunions, and funerals—all are events where we connect with one another. These are opportunities where we can connect with all that is sacred. Our awareness of the sacred intensifies when we creatively and intentionally listen for God's voice in biblical and living stories. Both ancient and contemporary stories provide a scenario that can teach us about ourselves and about our communities. We learn about ways others have waited for God and have experienced the miraculous. Stories also teach us about the complexity and virulence of oppression and of the many movements throughout history that brought freedom, justice, and equity to the huddled masses yearning to be free. With the call of God on our lives to do ministry, we totally embrace all that is holy as we make joyful sounds and gestures to the Lord in all that we do.

Responsive Reading 3

Leader: In living a spiritual life we embrace the religious character of our lives as a healthy context for our existence.

People: **As we sing and pray in worship we celebrate the mysteries of the Spirit that let us hear the interpretations that best minister to our souls.**

Leader: In renewing our faith and trust in God we lay out our doubts and fears as part of our journey toward wholeness and fulfilling God's call on our lives.

People: **As we confess and dance like David before God, we shout hosannas and alleluias, we lift holy hands, and we skip with joyous feet in praise.**

Leader: In drawing closer to God and honoring the God within ourselves we focus on that which is good, and work for the transformation of that which is not.

People: **As we read scripture and give our offerings we remember the blessedness of giving and receiving as we honor those who would give and cannot.**

Leader: In releasing our fears and our confusion we come before God's mercy seat, certain that God hears us, loves us, and will transform us.

All: **As we grow stronger in God and are no longer victim of our own emotions and habits, we give thanks for each new day that brings new possibilities.**

Sometimes we fail to grasp the religious nature of our lives. We do not realize that with each breath we connect to God's creative wind and energy. When we begin to grasp the depths of the sacred in us, our entire lives are liturgical: part of the God-given drama of worship and proclamation, which shifts the way we see, interact, and live. Then, certain behaviors are not acceptable. We come to know a daily sense of renewal and those times of conversion as life changing, on a level that connects to our bone marrow. In daily worship, all our gestures—handshakes, dancing, saluting, speaking, and sighing—become symbolic acts of praise. Daily worship means a closeness with God that moves us to another level of aliveness. In daily meditation and reflection, prayers and contemplation become rich, fluid minutes in time where the heavens and earth converge toward joy and peace unspeakable. A daily embracing of the sacred makes us aware of God's glimmers of grace—those times when we experience the beatific vision. Seeing and sensing *this* level of the sacred makes us sanctified creatures, blessed a hundred times over, able to do justice, to love mercy, and to walk humbly with God.

Responsive Reading 4

Leader: As individuals and as community, we offer thanks for the many blessings of God, which inspire a more faithful life in covenant.

People: **Blessed is the name of God, great and glorious, larger than the heavens and earth: all honor, praise, and joy be Yours.**

Leader: As individuals and as community, we know we need to heal: release our anger, fear, hurt, envy, lust, addictions, all behaviors that destroy us from inside out.

People: **Blessed be the names of our ancestors, of the prophets and the saints who pray for us, who have modeled the sacred life for us, and who love us still.**

Leader: We confess we have lived in denial and that we have not had the courage to stop destructive behavior, especially the daily violence that we hear in our own conversations.

People: **Blessed be the names of those martyrs, ancient and new, who have given their lives that we might live in a world of peace and love.**

Leader: As individuals and community, we open ourselves to God, that all things that need changing will be transformed, and that those things that need to stay the same will remain unchanged.

149

All: **Blessed be the names of the children, the youths, and the adults who depend on each of us for guidance, health, and strength, as we do ministry.**

For most citizens in the United States the word *Thanksgiving* connotes a major secular holiday that is scheduled for the fourth Thursday in November. This is a festive time when merchants heighten their Christmas marketing, the season when they sell over 60 percent of their merchandise. Today, Christmas goods are often in the stores by the end of October. Ultimately, Thanksgiving in its truest sense is not about a national holiday or time for a marketing blitz campaign. Thanksgiving is a mode of appreciation for blessing, an attitude or ritual of gratitude. How can we worship God in spirit and truth and not be grateful? We offer thanksgiving because of God's loving blessedness. An ethos of thanksgiving provides the room for confession, change, and healing. As community and individuals, we can embrace the opportunity to heal, knowing that we need not be vindictive, we only need love. Denial makes it difficult for some to be able to start with confession, admitting our wrongdoing. With covenant faith not only are all things possible, but we will have the strength and the courage to confess, repent, change, love, and grow toward nurturing a world of peace and love.

Prayers of Commitment

Prayer of Commitment 1

Gracious God, You are our light and salvation; into Your hands we place our health, spirituality, and well-being. We ask Your blessing for saving grace at home, work, and play, in our mental, emotional, physical, economic, and spiritual lives, together. Help us have the courage to try new ways of being, even when they seem risky and move us from our comfort zone.

Be with us as we take small steps toward honoring your image within. Bless us as we explore those parts of ourselves that shame us. Help us make amends and repair those past injuries that we have inflicted on others, those past injuries that we have done to ourselves. Forgive those past injuries perpetrated on us. As we examine these various injuries, help us name the pain, confess the wrongdoing, work through the grief and distress, and move toward healing. Let us face our enemies in a way where neither of us is crippled. Help us see clearly who we are and what people, places, and things are unhealthy for us. Grace us with a community of support when we embark on these dangerous missions. Bless us this day and thank You for such healing insight.

As people of faith, we pray for many reasons, in a variety of settings, alone and with a community of people. We pray that we might feel God's light and the joy of God's salvation. Having an active prayer life increases our health and well-being. When we pray frequently about all things, we heighten our sense of spirituality and our awareness of the many blessings God bestows on us. That heightened awareness permeates our lives and becomes a fluid part of our existence. A rich prayer life strengthens and sustains us and helps us live our lives with a greater sense of equilibrium. With this symmetry comes new ways of being, a change from having a life where it is always "a day late and a dollar short" to a life where there is always time for God's will for us. A life of equilibrium means experiencing day-to-day existence, as having enough time. We become prone to having fewer days where we book too many happenings and try to be too many things to too many people. A life of symmetry enables us to experience ourselves as being made in God's image, thus taking better care of ourselves. A life of equilibrium helps us ease the drama of our daily lives and resist any desire to self-destruct by doing bad things to ourselves. We have the courage to avoid people who are poisonous to our self-esteem, our well-being, our total health, and our balance.

Prayer of Commitment 2

Loving One, we know that secrets can lead to denial and destruction. In our quest for health and wholeness toward finding new ways of living a sacred life, we ask Your guidance, mercy, and care. Our woundedness is often so great that we find it difficult to face the truth about ourselves and our families. We fall prey to protecting the family name and to keeping bad situations hidden, and we often unintentionally cause more harm than good. Help us tell the secrets that harm humanity and keep us from getting well. Please give us the courage and a sense of outrage when we know bad things are happening so that You can lift the fog of denial and bring on the sunshine of reality. As parents, help us see our children as blessed gifts; help our desire to be good parents; assure that we will always love our children well. Help us let go of our children, when appropriate. Deliver us from needing and trying to clone our children into our own image so we do not try to live out our might-have-been lives through them. As children, help us see our parents as wonderful guardians of our faith. As a community, help us appropriately honor one another by learning to live together in harmony.

In doing ministry it becomes important to establish trust and respectful boundaries. Those who lead are called to listen prayerfully with discernment, and to serve as a guide when parishioners and others come with problems and secrets. Good secrets—wonderful news that one is holding in abeyance until the right moment—can be marvelous. Bad secrets—things we are ashamed of, feel guilty about, that depress us—are things that need to be confessed. There may be some secrets an individual does not feel safe or confident in sharing with any other person. At the least, we can always bring these kind of secrets to God in prayer. When we do not confess such information to God or another human being in confidence, the weight of it is devastating: bringing stress-related disorders, high blood pressure, depression, and so forth. God already knows our secrets and wants to love us, God's prodigal sons and daughters, back into health and wholeness. Confession releases us and relieves us from being frozen in denial. Confession is the practical experience of letting go and letting God. By exercising and stretching our prayer muscles we move toward a more balanced life, where we release guilt and poor living habits and we embrace God's grace and vitality.

Prayer of Commitment 3

As covenant people, we are called to value community participation, supported by faith, and lived by engaging in loving deeds.

152

As we value the mutual love and support made possible by You, help us remember those who may not yet know You. We pray for the homeless, those riddled with HIV/AIDS, cancer, depression, all stress-related disorders, and all those who have unresolved anger against themselves and the world. We look for new ways to celebrate our blessings and ask for Your anointing of the Holy Spirit and for peace. We rejoice in the little moments of joy and happiness that come our way. We bless ourselves and Your gifts of our lives that make it possible for us to see, hear, smell, touch, and taste infinite kinds of beauty. We give thanks for the magic of time, the ebb and flow of the great waters, for the light and dusk of day. We bless You for the order and symmetry, the ambiguity and the mysteries in the world, which often spark bursts of creativity reflected in art, music, and dance. May we use the talents and gifts You have blessed us with to be a blessing.

One of the blessings of being human is the benefit of being able to be an individual and also be a part of several communities. Only through divine grace can we fully participate in the sharing of love and care. We know that there are many things in this world that we cannot change. Yet we also know that collaboration can make a difference, and for those whose plight we cannot change, we can offer intercessory prayers on their behalf. One of the traditional African American spirituals says its well: "Prayer is the key children . . . unlock the heaven's door for me."[2] Through prayer we unlock the gates of heaven and earth as the Holy Spirit advocates on our behalf. With this level of empowerment and anointing we come to know the "peace that passes all understanding," that peace which is otherwise incomprehensible. This peace is attainable even in the midst of chaos and turmoil. With the power of the Holy Spirit we are no longer threatened by differences or by things we do not understand. With the equilibrium and symmetry that comes of an active prayer life empowered by the Holy Spirit, we become free to live in the beauty and majesty of God.

Prayer of Commitment 4

In recognition of all that is holy and sacred, we give thanks to God, Creator of all, knowing that creation is all one. The clouds

153

moving in the sky, the ripples in the creek, the plants pushing through the earth as seedlings, the prancing of animals, and the beating of our hearts: all are pulsations, life rhythms making divine music, and saluting all that is sacred. In the tranquillity of such moments we praise the Creator and honor the created. With fertility in spring and death in fall we offer our humble prayers of appreciation for the cycles in nature and the possibility of renewal. As all nature expands, shrinks, changes in so many ways, we see our own mortality, our largeness and importance, our smallness, and relationship to all of life. We abide in the majesty of God so that we can be responsible stewards regarding everything in our care, in our world. We know the challenge of living a balanced life and commit to realizing the notion of time, work, and rest, to the benefit of our various communities and ourselves.

To pray is to recite holy words in sacred ways. When our words and our bodies become one in prayer, we celebrate with thanksgiving all that God has created. As part of that creation, we are part of the rhythms of the universe: a symphonic masterpiece of vitality. If we are trapped and are overwhelmed with commitments and time constraints, if we are depressed and overburdened with the cares of the world, we will miss the blessing of knowing this godly vitality. We become so desensitized that we then lose track of the seasons of our lives and take life itself for granted. With faithful prayer we experience time as energy, and life as fertile with many new creations, and death with the culmination of greatness, in the realm of physical life. Prayer becomes complete after we become quiet and listen for God. When we hear God, we receive direction, love, and mercy. When we heed God, we respond with a heightened level of accountability and praise. When we attend God, we know the Holy of Holies, we become sacred, we live in a more balanced life, and we give thanks.

---

1. R. Laird Harris et al., *Theological Wordbook of the Old Testament*, vol. 2 (Chicago, Moody Press, 1980), 836-37.
2. See the traditional African American spiritual "Prayer Is the Key."

Chapter 8

Spirituality: Looking for a Way into Ourselves

Looking, seeing
Similarities, differences;
All shut eyes not sleep
All opened eyes don't see
Dealing with all or nothing
Strains one's sensibilities
Against the structures of our minds.

Stuff in, stuff out:
More garbage
Left diffused and unprocessed
Clanking around
In a head
Dismissed as having no value.

Singing sweetly, softly
Melodies of praise and joy
Opening currents of hope
Deemed valuable, noteworthy:
One human speaks with another
God listens and speaks:
Awesome, audacious:
'Cause God and somebody else cares.

*T*here are so many wonders that make up the human body, particularly the ability to see and have intense visual experiences. Those with the gift of eyesight know the magic of seeing varying hues of colors, textures, depth fields, sizes, and shapes in different dimensions. Sometimes those with eyesight look but ultimately are not able, capable, or willing to see. Those who are blind also have sight, a different kind of sight, but when experienced can be equally informative and inspiring.

155

The caution then is for us to not take our vision, our sight—physical, spiritual, or intuitive—for granted. Those who can look but cannot see are not to be ridiculed. Sometimes betrayal and the absence of love preclude us from fully experiencing the gift of seeing. Truly, all eyes that are open do not see. Discernment is crucial for clarity in interpreting and processing what we see, particularly when we are pensive, engaging in reflection, in looking inward.

Many books and articles have been written about adapting the contemplative or meditative life in monasteries to contemporary life. Many persons in religious orders and others on faith pilgrimages participate in weekend, sometimes month-long retreats that are at times, structured to involve many people. Sometimes people enter cloistered communities where they function in continuous silence. Those unable to visit a retreat center or monastery sometimes simulate the experience by spending part of a day in silence and meditation. One can develop a discipline that involves practices that provide meaningful spiritual food, inspiration, and a time of respite. That time may involve meditation, reading scripture, painting, music making, or gardening. One needs moments when one is quietly waiting for God. We cannot hear the call of God above the chatter of daily life.

Meditations

Meditation 1

Head pounding,
Muscles aching,
Ran out of time.
Actually, ran out on myself;
Put everything, everybody
Ahead of myself and my God, our God.

Eyes, bloodshot
Hands feel like carpal tunnel syndrome.
The heaviness of the day
Weighs more than
My thoughts about this moment
When I can connect with God
And what happens when I don't?

Clock ticking in the kitchen
Put on a pot of water
Boiling, steaming
Away my misery.

Misery brought from:
Working too hard, too intense:
Dealing with some things
That have no effect on whether
Folks at death's door
Soldiers in the middle of war
Homeless or disenfranchised beings
Know they are loved today.

Both the Hebrew Bible and the Greek New Testament contain several words that embody the concept of what it means to "look at" or the noun form, "a look." *Ra'ah* means to see, literally and figuratively; to behold, appear, discern, consider, perceive, or view. *Ra'ah* connects seeing to covenant remembrance, divine judgmental awareness, and a sense of human powerlessness when seeing. This term also pertains to two groups of unequal strength face-to-face; the blindness that can come of evil; and a cautionary note as to how and why one looks at another human (Gen. 9:16; Exod. 5:21; Deut. 28:32; 2 Kings 14:8; Ps. 40:12; Song of Sol. 1:6). *Nâbat* means to scan, look intently, to imply, to regard with pleasure as one sees the uncountable stars in the heavens; warnings about when not to look. *Nâbat* pertains to discovery; seeing in the face of another's death (Ps. 22:17). The metaphorical use of *Nâbat* connotes receiving and heeding directions; the anguish related to looking, not to seeing (Prov. 8:22); and a request to gain God's decision (Hab. 1:13). *Mar'eh*, a plural form, concerns how one beholds physical appearance (Gen. 12:11), especially if the one beheld is attractive (Gen. 26:7). The term also means to take special notice of (2 Sam. 11:2), especially beauty objectified (Esther 1:11), and to give a certain impression (Ezek. 23:15).

Pânâh means to face, to appear, behold, regard, respect, to look as one can disregard (Deut. 9:27). *Pânâh* also means to respect and recognize, particularly when one should be held in low esteem (2 Sam. 9:8); and to behold in context of truth telling (Job 6:29). *Pânâh* connotes a sense where one peers in a given direction, expecting the worst (Isa. 8:22); and concerns a call by the divine for humanity to focus on God for salvation (Isa. 45:22). Other terms in the Hebrew Bible pertain to the concept of looking, which include: *ro'iy*, a sight or abstract vision or concrete spectacle (1 Sam. 16:12). *Pâqad* means to visit, oversee, care for, deposit (1 Sam 17:18). *Kaw-vaw* means to bind, expect, collect, or tarry (Job 3:9; Isa. 8:17). *Châqach* relates to glance sharply, to peek (Isa. 14:16). *Tsaphah* means to lean forward, observe, await (Ps. 5:3; Mic. 7:7).

In the New Testament, *Blepo*, literally and figuratively, means to look at, look on, to behold, perceive, regard, see, take heed, sight (Acts 3:4; 2 Cor. 10:7; 2 John 8). *Prosdokaho* means to anticipate, to watch, to look for, to wait for (2 Pet. 3:13, 3:14). *Apekduomai* means to divest (Phil. 3:20; Heb. 9:38). *Skopeo* pertains to the sense where one considers, takes heed, or looks at (Phil. 2:4; 2 Cor. 4:18). Other terms, such as *optomai*, also convey that sense of gazing, appearing, seeing, to watch from a distance (John 19:37, Acts 18:15). *Ekdechomai* means to accept from some source, expect, look or tarry for, to wait for (1 Cor. 16:11). Thus, to look is an experience of multiple senses, of seeing, thinking, knowing, and understanding in particular ways, ways that can awaken a new and different kind of consciousness. Ultimately, the ability to choose to see is a gift. The opportunity to share this gift with others is one beginning toward inclusivity, respect, toleration, and joy in the midst of struggle.

Meditation 2

They didn't call the police
When he beat her, left her for dead.
They didn't get help
When she beat him with words, and then with a pot
Breaking his spirit, breaking his scalp.
They didn't call on God
For the courage to say stop—Don't be trippin'
Don't be hurting someone you didn't create
Don't hurt God's child.

They didn't call and neither did I;
I didn't call on God for myself
At the break of day or noon,
At the twinkling of the first star.
I and We and They took from God;
I and We and They take God for Granted.
I and We and They need to reconnect
And be responsible
And quit hurting others;
And quit hurting ourselves.

Are you going to call on God today?
I hear the rates are most reasonable;
That you can always get an appointment.
Did you call on God last night
Before you lay your weary head down
On the pillows of pain and hate?

When we call on God,
We hear a loving word;
When we call on God with others,
The Divine is with us and in us.
Are we going to call on God today,
Or do dreadful business as usual?

In the spiritual, social, and political fabric of the United States, we tend to hold to notions of manifest destiny and a Lone Ranger type of independence. Such attitudes give us credence to be concerned about our own interests and forget the gift of being a neighbor. Such minds often embrace a spirit of frontier sensibilities and a Darwinian survival of the fittest ethos. The problem remains that we do not listen to or for personal and communal pain. We forfeit our accountability for immediate gratification and omit the stewardship of a peaceful, balanced life. By claiming "it's not our business" we subvert the sensibilities of many faith traditions summed up in Jesus Christ's understanding of what it means to love one's neighbor as oneself. We cannot love, honor, or be in a healthy relationship with ourselves and a neighbor and not take some action when our neighbor is in pain. In such circumstances we must look into ourselves and acknowledge that we would want help if we were in the kind of pain that allows one to abuse and or to be the recipient of abuse.

Such analysis is not that difficult if one is in healthy balanced relationships. However, if one is in abusive relationships, as perpetrator or victim, then it becomes most difficult to identify the malfeasance. Garnering one's courage and seeing one's responsibility as a neighbor to take action may prove tedious, particularly with the move from thought to taking some kind of actual intervention. Fear and discomfort cannot paralyze us and stop us from acting in love to give assistance and support.

Meditation 3

A baby smiles, wrinkling its face
Like radar to sense where parents and loved ones are:
Sensing, connecting with all activity
In and around its little head
Making a joyful noise to God.
Hello everyone, Hello God!
I'm here; I'm alive
I need your love.

When we take on the innocence
The curiosity of an infant
We know God in a new and powerful way.
We renew our sense of awe and wonder.
Releasing the awkwardness and fear
That keeps us trapped
In lethargic pain
Making the walking dead.

Like a child, we have not learned
The lessons of life that always decry, NO!
Like a child, we know possibility,
We know discovery,
We know hope.

We trust someone cares for us.
We need not hear,

"Let go and let God."
As a child, this is the option we live,
The option we breathe;
The option that's true.

Healthy bodies, well cared for, are vibrant, innocent, curious, and vulnerable. They have a sense of awe and wonder as their personalities are forming, as they have not yet learned the crippling dimensions of "I can't." Innocent, infant joy knows of futures stamped with incredible potential. That potential basks in the eloquence of innocence as long as the adults around them honor their innocence, their curiosity, and their embodied love of God. A baby is a metaphor for the state of our openness, when we stand naked before God. Such a point of vitality and aliveness is unsurpassed: the dynamics vibrant; the possibilities immense. Such a state is the place of new beginnings and hope. Such hope invokes an opportunity for confession and absolution, for ultimate prayer, for trusting God, for becoming whole.

Meditation 4

Someone lives and someone dies;
Someone hopes and someone cries;
Someone forgives; others never forget.
In the moment of now, I have no regrets,
I only know God
I only know hope,
I begin to know me.

In the moment of now,
We breathe in the power of the Holy Spirit;
We dance, laugh, and shout with glee.
With all that God's done for us.
Life, a most powerful gift
We need not always then create rifts
Amongst friends and foe alike.

In the moment of now,
God, the I am, is the God who is becoming.

I and Thou in that moment:
Children in the becoming phase,
For the first moments, for the rest of this day
Are but signals of hope and joy
When God sees us, face-to-face, as we pray.

Different traditions experience time in a variety of ways. For many Buddhists, time is circular, is part of the process of enlightenment that embraces wisdom, boundless compassion, and total liberation.[1] For many Native Americans, time is fluid, is in the realm of the spirit; when things do not happen it was not the right time, as events begin when they are to begin—in line with the spirit.[2] In many African traditions the time for life spans the unborn, those that live today, and their ancestors who are physically dead but spiritually ever present. How we experience time shapes how we order our life, how we understand all creation, how we see the unexplainable, how we deal with issues like eschatology: traditionally the doctrine of last things or what happens at death. Alternatively, eschatology also relates to how one sets goals for this life, which imply how one relates to life after death.

The moment of most aliveness is the moment in which we live and breathe in present time. The moment in which we act, we experience the immediacy of life. In those moments of heightened reality and vital intimacy, we can make a difference. In these sharp, real moments, we know the essence of ourselves, we connect with the divine in others, and we experience hope, the empowerment of the divine, and the joy of freedom. Hope meets thanksgiving and creates nobility and peace. That which is noble is honorable and good. That which is of peace imparts serenity and wellness. In peace, our experience of time is a gift. That which knows health, wellness, and peace can know God.

Responsive Readings

Responsive Reading 1

Leader: Open O gates of heaven as we open our hearts to see God and see ourselves.

People: **We rejoice for the inner journey, for times of reflection and being quiet to better know God.**

Leader: In opening our hearts and spirits to love and renewal we confess all pain and guilt—all things contrary to the Holy Spirit.

People: **We rejoice for the inner journey, for the clarity of being fully present with ourselves in the spirit of creation and peace.**

Leader: Open your minds to receive the goodness of God, the goodness of yourselves, the goodness of created order and all that dwells herein.

People: We rejoice for the inner journey, for the wisdom that comes from longevity, for the innocence that embraces healthy childhood.

Leader: In opening our minds, bodies, and souls to the grace, mercy, and peace of God, we are made new each day, better equipped to love.

All: **We rejoice for the inner journey, a way of life that brings about contentment, balance, and joy in the seconds of each day as we live fully.**

There are many paths to an inner life of contemplation, prayer, and connectedness. Most of these paths require action. We tend to think of prayer and meditation as passive—they are not. Indeed, they involve quiet action or active silence. Developing a spiritual practice or discipline involves work, and the daily repetitions of that work, so that the disciplines become habitual, second nature. Second nature is not synonymous with static or passive but an ongoing commitment with little or no struggle. The practice of reflection, meditation, and prayer can become a part of our daily lives, and thus became effortless, though they require a spiritual space and a time commitment. One traditional hymn says it best: "Take time to be Holy." This invitation to be in frequent conversation with

God and the divine within is a journey, a pilgrimage, and perhaps an adventure—one that can bring peace, wisdom, and revelation, and can be life changing.

Such a life change can be a holistic experience of salvation. Some ask, "Can I lose my salvation?" How can one lose something that one never fully had? The experience of salvation is not simply that moment of realization when God as Savior, particularly, Jesus as the Christ, becomes a powerful presence in one's life. Salvation is an ongoing, daily encounter. Just as one cannot rely on the air breathed in 1990 to provide the necessary oxygen and other nutrients for life today, one cannot rely on the experience of grace received ten years ago to keep one in relationship with God today. The catalyst for the salvation experience is the Divine-human relationship. If one claims to be saved, yet hates, how can this be? If one claims to be born again, yet abuses others, lies, steals, cheats, manipulates on a daily basis, how can we possibly love God?

Responsive Reading 2

Leader: We lift our prayerful voices and thoughts to God in praise and gratitude, as we wait with joy to hear the still, quiet voice from heaven.

People: **For inner peace and the joy of being in relationship with our personal selves, we give thanks.**

Leader: In the moments of solitude we look inward to see God inside so that we can radiate God's presence and light wherever we go.

People: **For inner peace and the joy of loving ourselves, we give thanks as we learn to be our own best friend.**

Leader: In the moments of meditation we listen for the voice and wait for the presence of God to begin the healing process that builds on confession and forgiveness.

People: **For inner peace and the awesomeness of being fully present before God, unencumbered by things and deeds, we give thanks.**

Leader: In the moments of fear and doubt, we still listen for the experience of God, however God chooses to self-reveal to us, toward building a covenant connection with the one who creates, redeems, and heals.

All: **For inner peace and a more integrated self, for being a unique being among all those created by God, we give thanks to God.**

Language is such a beautiful instrument or vehicle for expressing love, artistry, and the sacred. Sometimes we get so caught up that we forget the power of "thank you," "you are welcome," and "good morning." We miss the blessing of ourselves. When in touch with this level of abundance and benevolence, we truly experience gratitude and intimacy at the level of relationship. Relationships hewn of peace and joy, by God, are the catalysts for balance and healing. When entering new relationships one of the first questions to ask is not *Will this person like me?* or *What do we have in common?* or *What advantages will this relationship bring me?* The first question to ask is, *Has God called us to be in this relationship, and if so, how might we honor such a covenant?* Such openness to God and openness to the ensuing growth that comes of such divine requires self-reflection in solitude. Sometimes these moments may be rife with terror: fear, doubt, and uncertainty. Sometimes in the valleys of dread and the shadows of death we finally meet God: we know what we are called to do. We finally can see our true selves.

Responsive Reading 3

Leader: In the beauty of God's majesty we are but one beam of God's light that radiates love and joy, letting us better see ourselves.

People: **In renewing our lives in God, we come to know ourselves better and are often surprised by the gifts, long buried, that rise up in praise of heaven.**

Leader: In the beauty of God's majesty we learn that God

does care. In the quiet moments of hectic days we feel a breeze and know God just passed by.

People: **In renewing our lives in God we find new hope and learn our own experience of what is healthy, what affirms us, what makes us whole.**

Leader: In the beauty of God's majesty we know an overwhelming sense of freedom, for we no longer apologize for who we are and whose we are.

People: **In renewing our lives in God we come to know and love ourselves.**

Leader: In the beauty of God's majesty we may be confused about many things, but we are incredibly clear about God's love for us.

All: **In renewing our lives in God we come to know a peace that sustains us amid the storm, that holds us when all is well, and that inspires us during the in between times.**

We often bandy about the language of renewal and spiritual development without dealing with the cost. To engage in being more godlike, to know oneself in a positive light, may be an opportunity or a vale of horror. Some people are out of touch with themselves or in great pain; there is a familiar sense of distance or hurt. Their lives resemble the tread of worn tires that barely leave a hint of their existence. The cost of knowing the generative light of God in their lives may be so disruptive that individuals may completely fall apart. They may lose all sense of reality and direction. In seeking God and their true selves, they may get lost. In most cases the loss is not so profound as to require long-term professional assistance. Sometimes the revelation of God and self can be so monumental that one will have to change one's life completely. Such transformation usually requires a new way of being, thinking, and doing. Such change could be as narrow as changing the way one manages time or finances to needing a complete makeover: new faith traditions, new occupation, new friends—a brand new life!

Responsive Reading 4

Leader: With each breath we take we inhale the grace and goodness of the Holy Spirit, buoying us up, above things mundane, on the doorsteps of hope.

People: **In the silence of a second God moves, cares, and loves, as angels bring good tidings of great joy to all people—that God loves us, that God is true.**

Leader: With each breath we take we embrace the nobility of the human spirit, and the compassion of the Divine.

People: **In the silence of a second we experience renewal, refeshment, and resurrection—a blessed quietness that rings loudly of grace.**

Leader: With each breath we take we daily prepare to honor God's worthiness, as each moment of life becomes an element, an encounter of worship.

People: **In the silence of a second we pray for the leaders of the world, for like each of us they stand individually before God, in fear, sometimes projecting their pain on us.**

Leader: With each breath we take we know hope and possibility, for each inhale and exhale is a praise and benediction, a blessing and a thank you, in honor and to the glory of God.

All: **In the silence of a second we hear the wind as spiritual music to our ears, knowing God's presence within every fiber of our being, making our bodies, our temples, sacred.**

The Spirit of God buoys us up like a raft floating on a calm sea. God's love and power is so vast yet gentle that when we are in tune we sense the energies that radiate from that love as gargantuan. The force of God's love can be as delicate as the smile of a newborn, as quick as the speed of light, as minute as a drop of water into the ocean. The impact of that same love can be as profound as the cascading torrents of Niagara Falls or as the remains of Pompeii after the eruption of Mount Vesuvius. The dynamics and aesthetics of such love transcend the beauty and splendor of all the flowers that have ever been feted during the Rose Bowl Parade in Pasadena, California, on New Year's Day.

The complexity and aesthetic sensibilities of creation are part of our reality, yet beyond our complete comprehension. Even for the most traveled, the most learned, the most experienced—we can only be in one place at one time. We can possibly know several sensations simultaneously, yet can only engage one text (book, play, story, song, scripture) in one moment, though we may have a historical memory of several texts in mind. Such matters of time and love and faith and knowing and health are concerns, both divine and human. Sometimes we cannot phantom a whole, just, healthy society because our categories are too small; our vision, too limited. Yet the sheer numbers of persons on the planet that care, that daily make a difference, gives credence for our believing and for doing justice, loving kindness, and walking humbly with God.

Prayers of Commitment

Prayer of Commitment 1

Gentle Spirit, we come before Your presence with thanksgiving and with the desire to know You better, and likewise, to know ourselves. We often fear the quiet time, for then all our doubts are exposed, our fears are raw. We dread the silence, in fear of what You might say and in fear of the acknowledgment of the times when we have betrayed You and failed to live up to the wisdom and other spiritual gifts that You have bestowed upon us. In Your eminent mercy, we come to know a joy unspeakable. Bless us that we may live in a manner that respects You, that respects ourselves. Come spreading Your undeniably awesome gestures on the part of creation. We bless You for the gift of silence and self-knowlege. We thank You for the gift of thinking, reflecting, and meditating amid Your mercy, love, and justice. For the gifts of illumination that come of entering into the sacredness of prayer, we are grateful. Be with us when dawn meets daylight, as Your revelations bless us.

The slogan for the United College Fund, formerly known as the National Negro College Fund, claims that "a mind is a terrible thing to waste." This phrase comes with certain assumptions: that thinking and being a human being are gifts; that human beings have the capacity to think and have value; that anything deemed waste is discounted and to waste something is undesirable. This phrase also assumes that people both have access to education and have a choice about what they want to learn. In some places in the United States and in other countries evidence shows that one cannot make such assumptions. The countless numbers of adults who cannot read and the hundreds of farm workers and undocumented persons who work for slave wages witness to the fact that even in the United States of America all persons do not have equal access and equal opportunity.

This reality calls us to look critically at what we claim to know, how and on what evidence we know, and is an indictment on the judgmental assumptions that arise regarding gender, race, class, age, and privilege. For those of us who are blessed with the faculties to think and the financial and spiritual support to gain an education, we are blessed. What are we compelled to do to see that others have similar opportunities?

Prayer of Commitment 2

In the nobility of silence and the sacredness of all creation, we count the ability to know You, O God, as abundant joy. We are grateful for the time to look inward and see You. We celebrate Your mystery and mercy, Your daring love for us, Your unquenchable hope for all. As we look inward we honor and praise Your name for the gift of forgiveness that allows us to confess our wrongdoings with a sense of liberation and possibility for righting wrong and for living a transformed existence. In respect for Your love and in humility that You choose to give Your love to us, we bow in joyful adoration and thanksgiving. We bless You for allowing the creativity to worship with timbrels and dance, with loud clanging cymbals. We worship You in meditation and quiet with vows of contemplation and silence. Loving Spirit, fix our hearts, eyes, ears, and all our senses that we might see, smell, touch, hear, and taste Your powerful presence. Fix us that we might experience a part of heaven on earth. Let us know You in this present moment of light, which radiates wherever Your children worship You, and live that worship outside the sanctuary, everywhere we go.

When a builder embarks on a renovation project several items must be in place: contract, permits, blueprints, money, work crew, materials, and for some jobs, the right weather. When we embark on a plan of looking inward toward spiritual renewal we also need to be prepared. We certainly have to engage critical listening and discernment so that we can know the Divine as our source. We must be conscious and willing to learn, that we might know a sense of our own human responsibility. We must also be willing to stand at the apex of the paradox between ambiguity or fuzziness and revelation or radiance. We can prepare for some of the renewal process by clearing our schedules of tasks that can be delayed or those to which we now need to say *No*. We can make use of familiar spiritual books and disciplines or begin a quest toward new, fulfilling practices. We can seek counsel with others. Most important, we need to be open to an ongoing process of valleys and mountaintop experiences. We need to stand naked before God, willing to be shaped and transformed, and willing to make the lifestyle changes necessary to nurture and maintain our newfound selves.

Prayer of Commitment 3

Gracious, Loving God, we come before Your presence to reflect on our relationship with You, to experience renewal in this moment of our faith, and to recommit to living a life of love. We invite You to help us create a sense of time where we can be still and know that You are God. We bless You and ourselves for our convenant relationships that gird our spirit and give us strength. We give thanks for the time to engage in covenant renewal. We give thanks that You reveal Yourself to Your children as you reclaim them as they work to maintain dignity, self-respect, and communal solidarity. We rejoice that we can recommit each moment of each day to living a life of love. We are glad for opportunities where we can love our neighbor and love ourselves, making it real that we love You. We pray to recommit even when we

*are stressed out, feeling defeated, vulnerable, and alienated from
the realities of our community life. In thanksgiving, we go forth in
hope and love to serve and be served, to honor and be honored, to
love and be loved.*

Many biblical stories depict the disturbances and the miracles that can happen when one stands in God's presence. Moses' countenance changed. Hagar saw and named God, the only person to have such a privilege in the Hebrew Bible and New Testament. Joseph experienced divine wisdom through dreams. Hannah was so deeply engaged in prayer that Eli, the priest, thought she was drunk. Lazarus returned from the dead. An unnamed woman's faith caused her daughter to be healed. Clearly, there are so many different ways that one can be conscious, aware of, fully alive in God's presence. The moments of illumination are available to us if we but look and see and taste and smell and touch the authenticity, innocence, and pleasure of God. For as we are made in God's image, we possess that same dignity and value and love. God is worthy to be praised. Each of us is worthy to be loved.

Prayer of Commitment 4

*God of life and health, we bless You for giving humanity the
gifts to create music and poetry, vehicles that aid us on our spiritual journey. We give thanks for the many kinds of music, the dramatic and majestic, the quiet and pensive, which move us along to
where we need to go. We know the blessings of beautiful constructions of words and phrases, as they too inspire. Give us the
strength and courage to be open to spiritual disciplines that
embrace who we are. Help us see the riches of self-expression honoring You, O God, that we might use them to bring us closer to
You. Help us honor time in our lives and help us be disciplined
enough to daily make contact with You, through prayer and meditation, through song and sermon, through being together in community as we balance the beingness and doingness of our lives. We
pray for inner peace and peace in the world, that strife and fighting decrease as active, empowering faith press us to love well.*

When we forget to laugh and be creative we cease to be

whole and healthy. Many of us are incredibly stressed because we have chosen a life that involves an occupation and other habits that are chaotic, troubled, and undisciplined. Such lives place us under such duress that we make ourselves sick. The sickness emerges from excess in too many areas: getting insufficient sleep, working too many hours, being committed to too many organizations, and spending too little time with loved ones, with self, and with God. We can begin to ready ourselves for renewal by studying our lives, and begin to downsize on all the things we do. We can make healthy decisions about how many hours we will work. This is a difficult one because with some jobs—especially in medicine, law, politics, education, and the entertainment industry—time is often not one's own. The issues become advancement or sanity and balance. Perhaps it does not have to be either/or; perhaps it can be both/and. How to accomplish this difficult change in institutional and personal mind-sets, attitudes, and expectations requires much thought, prayer, and negotiation. If reenvisioning our lives is important to us, we will devise a way to do so.

---

1. http://www.fwbo.org/buddhism.html
2. Conversation with Sonja Giles, Berkeley, Calif., June 1999.

Chapter 9

Spirituality: EGO (a.k.a. Engaging God Often)

Touching the omnipresence of God,
Creates a sense of wonder,
An explosion of amazement
Sometimes a quiet voice.
Other times a cacophonic, thunderous drum roll:
Resounding across the abyss of nothingness
Calling forth vital, effervescent beings.

Hearing the omnivocality of Spirit,
Holiness personified;
Triggers electrical sensations
Life's rhythms amid
Symphonic grace.
Bringing healing, forging health
Offering forgiveness and mercy
Reconciliation unspeakable
Praying chaos from ambiguity
Into community: diverse, holy, and sacred.

Seeing the omnigloriousness of Wisdom,
Engages God Often.
When our knowing is sacred;
Our being evokes justice:
Our tasting and speaking partakes divine ambrosia;
Our smelling experiences holy incense;
Our touching massages covenant intimacy
Our seeing envisions transformation
Moving division, hurt, depression, rage, fear, lust
Into a catalyst for change.

Some argue that connecting with God to connect with others is totally illogical and delusional, that God is a series of

173

grandiose projections of human beings who need a crutch to hold on to because of their benign neglect of their own human responsibility. Thus, folk who need a God are pathological; are crippled. Others make the Deist argument that God does exist and is not merely a human projection, but that God created everything at the beginning and has now taken a hands-off attitude. As those who believe in the gift of freedom, we must allow those thinkers room to believe what they choose to believe. Their belief system, however, does not negate the belief system of those who have an intimate relationship with God on a daily basis and who welcome an opportunity to connect with that part of God that resides in all humanity. In the moments of engagement with others, where divine sparks are united in community, one experiences the revelation and the manifestation in wonder, amazement, and thanksgiving.

Meditations

Meditation 1

The Breath of God
Spins within the universe
Fashioning humanity resplendent
In the image of I-amness
Coupling multiple I's:
Creating communal We's,
Of diverse cultures and sensibilities
Magnificently engaged.

The Breath of God,
The catalyst for life
Dances through our beings;
Empowered by grace.
Millions of gentle beings
Gifted with laughter
Harmed by violence
Confused by mixed messages
'Til heaven shines among us, now.

The Breath of God
Exudes the sacred:

Kisses our lips with hope;
Touches our hearts with joy
Hugs our pain to heal us
Laughs with us as ritual of renewal
Runs with us in celebrating innocence;
Argues with us—
That we may think.
Soars through us
To make us whole.

If we assume the existence, love, mercy, compassion, and justice of God, how do we know when we have made a connection? How do we know that we are not delusional, that we have not imagined those times when we thought we experienced God's presence? When we felt strangely moved, was it God or some distinct, unrelated neurological or psychological reaction? Many times individuals in the Bible experienced God. The revelation occurred through a theophany: a visible, often spectacular manifestation of God to a human being amid natural phenomena such as clouds and dreams, as well as messages within visions and by way of an angel, especially an angel of the Lord.

God often manifests or appears in the clouds, or a pillar of cloud, for a variety of reasons. God manifests in the cloud as the provision of light or cover for guidance, direction, and travel (Exod. 13:21-22; 40:35-38; Num. 14:14; Ps. 78:14). Some scholars note that the cloud as a "pillar of fire and a pillar of cloud," may pertain to the ancient practice of carrying a burning brazier, a pan for holding burning coals, to lead a caravan or marching army, indicative of the march by night and by day. The cloud also symbolizes God as the protector and warrior on behalf of the children of Israel (Exod. 14:24). The cloud is a realm of the revelation of God's glory (Exod. 16:10; 24:16; 1 Kings 8:10-11; Isa. 4:5; Ezek. 10:3-4). The cloud is the location from where God speaks (Exod. 19:9; 34:5; 40:34; Num. 11:25; 12:5; 16:42; Deut. 5:22), particularly during the Transfiguration (Matt. 17:5; Mark 9:7; Mark 9:35) when God claims the sonship of Jesus to Peter and James. The cloud is the realm of God that rests on the mercy seat (Lev. 16:2). The locus of the cloud indicates God's residency in a particular place (Num. 9:15-22).

God may come to persons through dreams giving messages of warning and blessing (Gen. 20:3-7; 28:12-17); and God may come through visions with messages of reward and of prophetic call (Gen. 15:1-21; Isa. 6:1-12; Ezek. 1:1-3). In scenes that were the forerunners to any of the visual stellar portrayals of Cecil B. DeMille, Steven Spielberg, and George Lucas, God appears within a burning bush (Exod. 3:1-12). Other times, God's manifestation occurs through an angel or embodied as an angel(s) relaying blessing and obedience (Gen. 18:2, 10, 13; 22:10-12, 15-18; Exod. 3:2-6, 14, 18; Judg. 2:1, 5). In some instances the text makes it clear that this deity amid the theophany is God (Gen. 16:9-12; Judg. 6:22-24; 13:21-23); and in the process the divine form claims the name of God (Gen. 31:11; Exod. 3:2, 6, 14). Some appearances of angels are directly related to the Christ event—that is, the coming, birth, life, death, and resurrection of Jesus, the Christ (Matt. 2:13, 19; Luke 1:11). As part of their tasks, angels, as messengers, do the work of God and proclaim the word of God.

When one comes in tune with God, particularly the Holy Spirit, one is better able to hear, see, and know various manifestations of God. Some experience God's presence as a living force in their lives. Others actually hear words of knowledge from God as prophecy and as answer to prayer. Some know God in the majesty of Creation and in their ability to create magnificent works of music, poetry, novels, and song. Others see God when they gaze out across the many terrains within our universe. Some experience God in the daily miracles of life itself as we are born, live, function, and engage with ourselves and others. Like Leonard Bernstein, some know God best in the simple things, in simple songs, "for God is the simplest of all." Amid this simplicity is great complexity, mystery, and that which can never fully be known.

Meditation 2

Our opened eyes
Like camera shutters
View pictures of our world, without, within:
Showing the interconnectedness
Of Creation, of Life, of God.

Daily see the mysteries
Dancing about us;
Visions of paradox.

Visions of faith;
Visions of hope personified
Visions of God weeping bitterly,
When we ignored any child;
When too hurried, too tired,
Open eyes did not see.

Our opened eyes
Scanning, seeing, knowing.
Those blind
Also scan and see and know
In different ways:
Heightened sensory indicts
The taking of things for granted;
Inspired the quest to
See, be, do in different ways;
Amid the daily moments of sacredness,
As we choose to love.

Our opened eyes
Are opportunities, a cornucopia of miracles.
When daily we celebrate
The sacredness of all life:
Oh, how awesome, how keen
When we but look and know in the looking
Occurred the sacredness of Grace.

Students of photography know the importance of lighting, distance, depth, colors, focusing, and on seeing as the camera sees, not how we would like the camera to see. Once the picture is recorded on film it can exist for time immemorial. One of the fascinating experiences one can know is to have several photographers shoot the same scene or individual in the same time frame. No two photographers will capture the same exact image(s) on film. Even when a photographer shoots two rolls of film of a model in order to get the most flattering photo-

graph for use as a head shot for a client's publicity and adver-
tising campaign, several different images of the client will
emerge in the sixty-four snapshots. How can this be? The pho-
tos say a lot about the client and a lot about the photographer.
Both persons are simple yet complex, and bring many experiences to the photo session. The openness of one's mind, body,
and spirit shifts from moment to moment. Each person is made
up of generations of combinations of genes, events, and memories. One comes to the session with thousands of images having been imprinted within one's being. With this much data
within us, how can we not but convey a different part of ourselves with each click of the camera? Given the complexity of
our lives and experiences of others, we must make room to
sense God's presence and to open our eyes to see and know on
a deep level. When we open our eyes, despite our joys and sorrows, our doubts, desperation, and fears, we have an opportunity to know sacredness, to become an integrated self: a self
who can see God in others, a self who can see God within.

Meditation 3

Engaging God Often
Becomes too expensive for those:
Drowning in high drama of being persecutor or victim;
Impaired by their own stubbornness
Dampened and depressed by circumstances
Stuck in ignorance,
They don't seem to know exists.

Engaging God Often
Becomes too traumatic
and not desirable for those:
Who have to do it "my way, or no way!"
Who see no options for change,
Who cannot see for looking,
Who are trapped by "what ifs,"
Who live in constant denial,
Who have never known love.

Engaging God Often
Becomes a blessing for those:
Who know their divine createdness,
Who want to learn to love,
Who can love themselves and others,
Who want daily connection with God,
Who experience prayer.

The expense and trauma of "Engaging God Often" can be so paralyzing to some that they can never move to another place. The need to be in control or have all the answers often pushes those who need to control to an untenable position, between a rock and a hard place, with few options to find a soft cushion. The ultimate discomfort of such a location becomes manageable because it is so familiar. There are risks remaining in this place—of becoming bitter, despondent, hopeless, unfeeling, or hard. God and the rest of society become the ones to blame for an unsatisfactory life. God and society become the scapegoats for one's righteous indignation, which can result in metastasizing anger and fear, along with physical, spiritual, and emotional atrophy or wasting away. Conversely, the discipline and practice of connecting daily with God and others who walk a spiritual path is a great blessing. Such connections unleash new creativity and genuine experiences of love. This daily connection does not produce arrogance, but self-assurance and ultimately, humility and energetic grace. One is able to love God in most profound, caring, and passionate way. One can love the many manifestations of neighbor unconditionally, in ways that move us to effect global transformation.

Meditation 4

How come? Why didn't they?
Questions after the fact,
Puzzle our minds and
Scramble our thoughts:
Amidst the simple; the complex.
We fixate on the paradox,
Unaware that the we-ness of paradox
Reneges on promises implied
By virtue of community.

We used to! We ought to!
Negations trapped in history—
Undercutting reality;
Bent on making a point
Of relevance
To pompous thoughts of Top Dog:
Standing in the tension of
Yesterday, today, tomorrow
Breaking connection with
the Ever-present sacred.

Yes we can! I want to!
Evokes the possibility
Of knowing divine immediacy
In the crucible of eternity
Juxtaposing: historical memory
Dead pasts; present elations;
Dreaded eschatons.
Breathe in the now: and know God.

Sometimes we belabor a difficult situation by asking too many questions that are ultimately irrelevant to facing what transpired and not helpful toward rectifying the present and experiencing transformation in the now, toward transcendence in the not yet but soon to transpire. Should we ask questions? Of course. Must we learn to live with space for mystery and ambiguity? Absolutely. In the process of asking questions about why things happen, we may discover that we can uncover no rational answers. When examining difficult, heinous, or bizarre occurrences that cause the suffering of the innocent, some rail back in response, "There is no God!" Others may say, "God was in the midst, suffering with the victims." Others may respond, "It was God's will." At the end of the day, and according to one's view of the world and creation, all these answers may be unsatisfactory. The reply that God does not exist is probably an honest response by someone who has not had a conversion experience or a spiritual life that has sustained him or her through times of joy and sorrow. They may have experienced so much pain that there has been no evidence of a substantive Divine that merits worship. Some ascribe a humanist approach, noting that all harm and pain exacted by human beings is the result of a lack of human responsibility and accountability. Others take comfort in knowing that God was there amid the suffering as natural disasters occurred or as some human beings made choices to maim or destroy human life. The response that seems most pathological and unseemly is the one that notes, "It was God's will." Why would a loving God desire torture, mutilation, or the destruction of human life and dignity? Perhaps we can learn and grow in ways that move us toward more neighborliness, dampening the need to control, to manipulate, and to kill the minds, bodies, spirits, and lives of God's chosen: all of God's children, even those without traveling shoes.[1]

Responsive Readings

Responsive Reading 1

Leader: Illustrious God, who desires relationship, we acknowledge Your love and witness to us in creation.

People: **As created beings we look to You, the Author and Finisher of our faith, as the source of our strength and joy.**

Leader: Illustrious God, who desires relationship, we honor Your mercy as a mirror that reflects the way we can live in community.

People: **As created beings we thank You, Beloved Creator, for Your magnificence, concern, and wisdom.**

Leader: Noble God, who crafted and fashioned each of our fingers and toes, we look to You for daily nurture, help, and strength.

People: **As people of God we lean on You, our Creator, Redeemer, Sustainer, for daily sustenance, guidance, and hope.**

Leader: Noble God, who crafted and fashioned the mountains, the trees, and the lilies of the field, we appreciate our immediate and eternal access to You.

All: **As people of God we look to Your spirit and strength, as the reservoir of life and well-being.**

Our experiences of many life issues could be very different if our perceptions and attitudes were different. When we operate from a base of love instead of woundedness, we cease to have a knee-jerk reaction to our perceptions of pain and injustice. We transcend the craggy depths of victimhood, to love ourselves and seek out those who can reciprocate. With a balanced life where our faith, health, and spirituality are in harmony, we see the love of God and can be God's witnesses everywhere we go. We then have an opportunity to honor the Creator and be honored as part of the created. We are able to be in relationships that caress and nurture us while stretching and challenging us. Such balance provides the impetus for unleashing our divinely given gifts of mercy and compassion. Each day we live, each moment we breathe, becomes an opportunity for giving thanks. This is not to say that we cease to have problems and that everything is positive and great. A balanced life, however, gives us a clearer perspective, a spirit of generosity, and a more level sense of ourselves and our communities. With a more balanced view of life we are able to be more sensitive to who we invite into our lives, honoring necessary boundaries and carefully selecting the kinds of activities we ought to engage in, because we are called by God to live, love, and do ministry.

Responsive Reading 2

Leader: On our journeys of faith and hope we come individually and in community to the mercy seat.

People: **In thanksgiving we daily bless ourselves and look to You, Loving God, to sustain ourselves and to bless others.**

Leader: On our journeys of love and faith we are both strong and weak, in word and deed, amid our covenant faith.

People: **In thanksgiving we offer our prayers on waking, at noon, at eventide for the gift of life and the gift of our relationship with You.**

Leader: As our faith and hope inform our health we rejoice that we are more mindful of You, of balances, and of the connections in all life.

People: **On our faithful journeys of life we often fall short, are envious, arrogant, fearful, and mean.**

Leader: As our faith and hope inform our health we give thanks for Your wisdom and love, for Your strength and joy that makes us whole.

All: **In our faithful journeys of life we yearn and desire health and life, framed by Your life and compassion for us.**

Just as we seek connectedness and balance in our lives, we want to be clear that our lives are rooted in God. A life of balance that meshes faith, health, and spirituality is a life framed by the fire, passion, and compassion of God. The fire warms us and energizes our bodies to breathe and exist as an independent entity, within community. For those with various challenges, their bodies are no less fired up, no less important. The divine passion or enthusiasm for life has been infused in us from the beginning of creation. Sometimes we forget and take life for granted because we become so whipped and battered by the daily stuff of life. Yet the times when we can hold fast to this passion are the days that we can laugh at ourselves and get right back upon the bicycle after falling off. Such laughter is not ridicule but a healthy release and a realignment of our body chemistry that can jar us back to a mode of accountability and "I will give it my best shot, regardless." Because of God's mercy, kindness, and justice, we can be kind and merciful and just. We can embrace our pilgrimages and our journeys with a sense of renewal and healthy desire. This desire is not the destructive kind that needs to subvert everyone else for the benefit of self. This desire, grounded in love, helps us imitate God and make a difference.

Responsive Reading 3

Leader: As we sing and pray we enter into a faithful experience of the light, openness, and freedom.

People: How magnificent are the moments when we focus on You, most holy God; moments of calm, peaceful existence with the rest of the world.

Leader: As we listen we enter into a faithful, humble knowing of joy, clarity, and oneness in community.

People: **How magnificent are the expressions of worship that remind us who we are; moments of centering, wholeness, and anticipation.**

Leader: As we kneel and bow down we become a part of the church universal, the millions of prayers, songs, sermons, and responses offered to Your glory.

People: **How magnificent are offerings of ancient and modern sounds in praise, when two or three or thousands gather together in Your name.**

Leader: As we enter and as we leave the sanctuary we come and go with Your blessings, to enter into worship; to go out to serve.

All: **How magnificent are You, O God, and all of your handiwork. In honor and praise, we shout glory! Hallelujah! Amen! Ashé.**

Numerous hymns, anthems, spirituals, and gospel medleys celebrate the awesomeness, magnificence, and the sufficient nature of God's grace. This grace, this power lived out, is a process that moves us through a continuum of great action to passive observance and prayer. Even in the moments perceived as passive we know a quiet energy as our blood and God's spirit courses through our bodies, bringing nutrients and inspiration. When illness, disease, or angst invade our beings we sometimes experience a fractured sense of self and reality. These are the times and moments for prayer, reflection, and realignment with the support of health practitioners, persistent praying folk, and our own cooperation. Many times we are victorious and we experience healing, even after long bouts of illness. Sometimes our health is not restored, but we reach an optimum level of existence. Sometimes people die. Death is not a failure of medicine, prayer, or belief. Death is death, a door that closes on one phase of life to open to yet another. Some are so paralyzed by myriad kinds of pain that they are the living dead. For these persons, we must pray and provide a healthy environment where they can help name and exorcise their ills. For those blessed with health and strength, each day is a time for excitement and quiet, for activity and hiatus. There are times for the "I love yous," the "thank yous," the "I need yous." These are times for creating sanctuary and tapping into the holiness of now.

Responsive Reading 4

Leader: In life we connect with one another as mirror images of who we are, who we can be, and who we are afraid to be.

People: **With eyes of heaven and earth help us see one another spiritually, with discernment, and a nobility of genuine concern.**

Leader: By God's grace we connect with ourselves and others in respectful ways, lovingly, so that we no longer "see through the glass darkly."

People: **With eyes of heaven and earth help us make healthy connections that build true relationships that nurture us and help us grow.**

Leader: As we see mirror images of ourselves in others help us love that which we dislike in ourselves and refrain from projecting our discomfort on others.

People: **With ears of yesterday and today help us appreciate spiritual traditions, yet have the courage and willingness to grow and change.**

Leader: As we see growth and healing in others help us acknowledge their wellness with goodwill, honoring God's beloved community.

All: **With ears of today and tomorrow help us embrace this day, plan smartly for the future, and have no regrets about the past.**

When doing spring cleaning or the grand opening of a new building, the windows are cleaned until they sparkle. In some large complexes, doors made primarily of glass are marked so that someone will not mistake a pristine glass door for an open passageway. When looking through such squeaky-clean glass doors one has a particular perception. If the door in that same passageway is scratched, smudged, or greasy, the perception shifts. The same experience occurs when we examine our lives and the lives of others. If we look through a clear glass window or clean, intact mirror, we see in a particular way. If we see ourselves through dirty, warped glass windows or through a broken, cracked mirror, the picture looks different. Our perceptions also depend on recent and old unhealed beliefs about ourselves and about life. Perhaps rather than peering only through new pristine glass or old cracked glass, one might look through both. Sometimes when viewed through old lenses, the warts, scars, or pimples on the face of our souls are not so bad. Yet when viewed through a shiny new glass door, we get to see how marvelous God has made us. When viewing from a balanced perspective, we see who we are, where we have come from, and often gain insight on where we need to go.

Prayers of Commitment

Prayer of Commitment 1

In quiet longing for Your grace and for a temperate joyful life, we say thank You. We lift up our eyes, our hearts, our voices, and our souls, forging an incarnational offering of love and thanksgiving. We pray for the courage to assume our responsibilities as Your children, called to love, share, and make a difference. We honor You for Your love and blessings upon us. We desire to be faithful and deliberate in living out our faith. We desire to be more loving and to interweave our faith commitment in every aspect of our lives. We pray for the gift of being conscious of You in the moments we deem insignificant and important. We welcome the opportunities to be aware of Your presence when gazing at tree bark or at a child crossing the finish line in the Special Olympics. We give You thanks for all those who see their lives as ministries that give and receive. We remain open to Your divine wisdom, that we might live our lives with divine energy toward transformation, wholeness, and a respect for differences.

One of the beautiful experiences of petitioning God through prayer is that, as the psalmists knew, we can trust that we have been heard. Here is one time when we know that the longing of our hearts is known by a Lover of deep commitment and fierce intensity. Some things we long for are frivolous, some even deleterious to our health. But the longing for God and the desire to connect with others in love are the seeds of a grounded, spiritual life that has great depth and inspiration. Such longing honors God and honors humanity. From the longing comes deep commitment and compassion. From the commitment and compassion comes the teaching, preaching, and living out of grace, where everyone has a voice and has a special place on earth. A utopia you say? Is it not more desirable to long for harmony than to long for hate? Although we may not be able to affect immediate global change, imagine the difference if, as we began to model such commitment and compassion, that others would recognize this and begin to do likewise. We would have the makings of a spiritual domino effect! Such "impossible possibilities" only remain such when we fail to relish our compassion and commitment in real ways.

Prayer of Commitment 2

God of mystery and tolerance, we welcome Your presence to us this day. We know that You never leave us or forsake us, but sometimes we forget and forsake You. We get so caught up in the doingness of life that we forget who we are, who created us, and why we have the gift of life. Bless us today with insight and a longing for being in concert with Your desires for Your creation. Help us embrace life's mysteries and the situations that make no sense to us. Guide us in being more tolerant of ourselves and others. We thank You for the blessings of mystery and how they remind us that we are not in charge and that we can never have all the answers. We celebrate with You the gift of humor and how it releases hidden tensions, which cripple us. We relish this gift of humor that builds community, healing, and brings balance to our lives. We honor Your gift of humor that helps us see how ridiculous we can be when we engage in unnecessary stress, and helps us laugh at our own shortcomings so that we can begin to make important changes for a well-rounded spiritual and healthy life. We rejoice that humor and laughter change us physically, mentally, and spiritually, enabling us to love ourselves and to share balance with others.

At the end of the day, when it seems everything has gone wrong, deadlines were missed, people misbehaved or performed poorly, and we got a ticket when the meter expired while doing someone a favor, we wonder how could this day have been different. We feel like everyone and everything would have been better off had we simply rolled over in bed, turned off the alarm, and gone back to sleep. Maybe yes; maybe no. We know that hindsight is 20/20. Thus, the question remains: What do we do today so that today does not unfold like yesterday, or if the same series of events occur, at the least, the day will not feel so devastating? Often we get trapped in the doingness of our lives, jobs, and relationships, and forget to experience them anew each day. Other times we forget that we are not God, thus we take our own viewpoints as gospel and law, and get outrageously perturbed at the audacity of any who dance to a different beat. Sometimes we are overwhelmed by our own human frailty and the large amount of pain and injustice that exist in the world. One of the marvelous things about God's grace is that as we can release all our cares, in praise and thanksgiving—admitting that we have no power over anything—we become powerful! With this power comes the ability to know joy and to laugh despite circumstances. As the act of releasing becomes a worshipful, spiritual experience, we can confess any complicity on our part and begin the process of being open to God.

Prayer of Commitment 3

Blessed Creator, we are so excited by Your love and care for us as we daily see the unfolding of Your grace. In things mundane and great, our time with You is like a great banquet, a tremendous feast. Prayer becomes a table laden at special holidays with all kinds of foods and special dishes. The more we pray, for others and for ourselves, the more we are fed. Each time we pray is like a separate dish or course. For those who face hunger and are homeless and in need, please make us more conscious of their plights and help those assisting them do so with dignity and humility. For those of us blessed with enough to eat, help us partake of our meals as sacred privilege. Help us be willing to eat the foods that nourish us, in the amounts that will not make us unhealthy. Help us realize that the nourishment of our bodies is a sacred task, as our bodies are our temples. May we be generous in giving nourishment through food and prayer to others who stand in need. For the harvests and the workers, we give thanks. For those who transport, distribute, and sell foods, we give thanks. For those who dispense spiritual food, we give thanks and ask for mercy. May we all know the gift of life, the gift of food, the gift of prayer.

Not only is prayer like a banquet, but in different ways it is also like partaking of breakfast, lunch, dinner, and any healthy snacks in between. Our morning prayers are like breaking a fast, the time from our evening talks with God through slumber to the next morning. We break the silence and start our day by saying, "Good morning God, here we are! Thank you for another day of living!" Some persons dread the morning because they wake up to distress or pain. Some cannot embrace God's glory because they feel betrayed by their bodies, by life, by God. Others remember the times when they were not in such pain, and praise nevertheless. There are no simple words that can allay this pain, but we can pray that those in pain can yet know peace. We can work harder on preventative mental, emotional, physical, and spiritual health for ourselves and our communities. We can pray for the discoveries of lifestyles, spiritual practices, and medication that can help alleviate pain. Prayer is like lunch: a time during midday to take a break to nourish ourselves and offer praise. Prayer is like dinner, a time to gather with others and express gratitude for the day. The whole day becomes a time for thanksgiving and intermittent prayer for ourselves, our communities, and for all beings in the world, that we may work, live, and exist together in better harmony: each one blessed, each one less stressed, each one loved.

Prayer of Commitment 4

Merciful One, we acknowledge Your care and Your concern for us and Your call for a Sabbath. Help us honor Sabbath during our daily lives so that we may slow down long enough to experience You in life and stop to take time for rest. Just as stop signs help moderate the flow of traffic on city streets, we too need to hear the stop signs in our lives that call us to halt and be in Your presence. Often we fear the vulnerability of standing naked in Your presence without busy work, tasks, or the drama that we create to avoid facing You and the reality in which we live. We pray for the experience of peace where the tensions of daily life cannot stifle or intimidate us. We embrace the joys of life that You give us as we build community and grow in spiritual strength and hope. May we appreciate the gift of Sabbath with anticipation for renewal and discernment. May our practice of Sabbath engender us finding healthy ways to rest. May we know Sabbath in the stillness and quiet of solitude. May we inhale Your Gracious Spirit and release that which is cumbersome, extraneous, and harmful.

Depending on our birth circumstances, childhood, teen, and adult life experiences and choices, some of us live the life of a roller coaster: steep uphill climbs and fast downhill lunges, with exhilaration or terror at every bend. Some of us have lives that resemble an airplane ride that hits occasional turbulence and may even skid at a landing or two, but the trips, at least to the passengers, feel pretty uneventful. Our take on the matter might be different if we were the pilot or a flight attendant. At times some of us live in the amusement park on the roller coaster; other times we sit in the plane among the clouds in comfort; and sometimes we are somewhere in between, on slow boats, on carriage rides, on bicycles, perhaps on feet. Whichever mode of transportation best symbolizes our life experience, we are not alone. We can fly comfortably because hundreds of people stand in the shadows making it possible for us to arrive safely. In all instances there are companies, designers, engineers, chefs, painters, mechanics, inspectors, programmers, and all kinds of fuel-efficiency and safety experts who service items and sign off on vehicles and equipment before they are deemed fit for public use. With the airlines, after the delivery of the jet plane, hundreds of persons from the travel and ticket agents, pilots, and attendants to the caterers, luggage handlers, and mechanics must do their jobs if we are to have a pleasant trip. Given our dependency on so many communities, perhaps we really need to honor a sense of Sabbath in our lives and pray that others will do the same.

---

1. See Maya Angelou, *All God's Children Need Traveling Shoes* (New York: Vintage Books, 1991). Also note the African American spiritual "I Got Shoes," a jubilant song, which uses irony to signify the reality that those singing who do not have shoes now are not victims, but will have shoes one day in the future.

Chapter 10

Wholeness: Faith Integrated with Health and Spirituality

Threads of life
Rivers of Respect
Moving, signifying potential.
Weaving of minds, souls, bodies
A conflagration of logic and mystery;
A glimpse into nostalgia
A dream about tomorrow
Whose lives, however,
May have time for neither.

Fibers mingling, holding, compressing
All that we are into bundles of sanctuary.
Each experience a quantum strand
Of story, of myth, of truth.
Sometimes compounded by lies;
Sometimes liberated by love;
Make up who we are:
Beings created by God,
Called by God to love and community,
Goodwill, and thanksgiving.

Faith motifs all about:
Tease us gently into that realm,
Of holding us to things hoped for,
To the evidence of things not seen.
Moving us to:
Surpasss vengeance and victimhood;
Overcome pettiness and punishment;
Release the bonds of things and fame
As fleeting moments of transcendence:
All that is left is love.

*F*aith, a dynamic energy that propels us through our day, is central to an experience of good health and spirituality, as a whole person. Faith helps shape our attitudes, which have a tremendous impact on our total health—mental, spiritual, emotional, economic, and physical. With faith we believe we can grow, change, and make a difference. With faith our attitudes are open. Thus the cup is half full, symbolizing possibility and a sense of movement toward reaching a goal, as opposed to a cup half empty, signaling a sense of loss, defeat, and trouble, trapped into being a victim. In the larger scheme of things, then, faith interweaves our life experiences, creating quantum strands of memories and stories about our walk with God, and our lives in the communities that have helped sustain our relationship with God. Faith serves as a catalyst for facing the impossible and for staying with a process, despite the obstacles that seem to block our way. A faithful spirituality provides the categories where we can sort out our decision making, make choices, dream dreams, and have visions about where God wants to take us.

Meditations

Meditation 1

Faith embraces the uncomfortableness of difference:
Shaking our realities,
Moving us out of those zones
Where we know everyone and everything,
Where we take God, ourselves, and everyone else for granted.

Faith concerns showing up and embracing
Those we despise,
Those who despise us,
Those who pretend we do not exist;
Embracing them not out of masochism,
But out of God's unconditional love,
Which allows us to love without being harmed.

> *Faith is an attitude adjustment, a process:*
> *That fuels our lives*
> *And gives us hidden power;*
> *That forms bridges over cavernous abysses,*
> *That defines new spaces where we can dwell,*
> *Protects us and lines our prayer closets,*
> *Helps us love and keep on loving.*

As we come to know faith and are able to embrace situations and individuals with unconditional love, and are able to make the adjustments that come of acceptance and forgiving ourselves and others, we know thanksgiving. In the Hebrew Bible, *towdâh, yâdâh,* and *huyʿdâh* connote thanksgiving. *Towdâh* relates to *yâdâh,* which literally means to use the hand, to throw, to worship or revere, with extended hands; to confess, praise, give thanks, thanksgiving itself. According to noted biblical theologian Claus Westermann, thanksgiving is a kind or form of praise.[1] A vow of praise is often a part of a communal lament, a time of sorrow and mourning, where a group feels threatened. *Towdâh* pertains to the offerings of thanksgiving related to sacrifice of unleavened cakes, and of well-being as listed in Levitical laws (Lev. 7:12, 13, 15). Thanksgiving involves singing in the midst of praying for deliverance (Ps. 26:7), or singing in praise of God's universal power and providential care (Ps. 147:7). Thanksgiving is a time for making thanksgiving the actual sacrifice instead of presenting a food item (Ps. 50:14; 116:17). Thanksgiving is part of the praise that elevates the name of God (Ps. 69:30), or thanksgiving occurs in God's presence (Ps. 95:2). *Towdâh* is an attitude one should have when entering God's court to praise (Ps. 100:4), and is related to the symbolism of creation and to end times (Isa. 51:3). Thanksgiving is also an appropriate response to restoration (Jer. 30:19).

In the New Testament, the major term for thanksgiving, *eucharistia,* and for thanks, *eucharisteo,* invoke giving favor, gratitude, to be grateful, to give thanks. In the Gospels, Acts, and Revelation, *eucharisteo* pertains to a thanksgiving prayer (John 11:41; Acts 28:15; Rev. 11:17), and notably, for thanks given at a meal (Matt. 15:36; Mark 8:6; John 6:11, 23; Acts 27:35). The terms *eucharisteo* and *eulogeo* (to speak well or to speak well of someone, which also means to extol, to praise, to eulogize) are often used synonymously. The use of *eucharisteo* regarding the miracle of the loaves and fishes is not yet to be viewed as the Eucharist, as in the Lord's Supper, though this interpretation arises later.[2] In the letters of Paul, a greeting of thanksgiving begins the Epistles and Paul includes thanks in the body of the letter. He gives thanks to God, the Creator, and speaks of giving thanks as the theme of worship, particularly in concert with prayer and praise and in relation to the increase of God's glory (1 Thess. 5:18; 2 Cor. 9:11). Thanks, in connection with God's glory, occurs in either a general exhortation or for a special reason, as in a collection for the Gentile churches.[3] Not only does grace increase with thanksgiving (2 Cor. 4:15), but when one gives generously, one is enriched and ultimately produces thanksgiving to God (2 Cor. 9:11).Thanksgiving or *eucharistia* is the context for prayer and supplication; instead of worrying, one can give thanks (Phil. 4:6). Part of being in spiritual relationship is to devote oneself to prayers of thanksgiving (Col. 4:2). When leading benediction and giving blessings, one does so singing *Amen!* with thanksgiving and honor to the glory and power of God (Rev. 7:12).

Meditation 2

Faith is a place that allows us to hold uncertainty;
Faith lets us stay where we are not wanted—
Until God tells us to move.
At such times, faith lets us release
All toxins targeted to kill us.
Faith is an antibiotic to stay the viruses of sin.

Faith is the ark of deliverance,
The underground railroad,
The source for all journeys from bondage.
Faith that celebrates chaos and peace,
The energy of change, and the results of reconciliation.

Faith embraces all things and nothing:
And God's choice to love us unconditionally.
Faith generates life

195

For those who want to live.
Faith opposes denial
For those who want to get well.

Faith is not an abstract thought or design and is not a mindless recipe for false piety. Faith, by definition, cannot be static. Faith is multifaceted, at once a place, an attitude, a process, a way of being, and a mighty connecting link between humanity and God. The place of faith is that realm of safety amid trouble, the location where we can yet hold to belief, and find assurance despite doubts and desperation. Faith is an attitude that lets us persevere even when it seems like we are getting nowhere fast. Faith is a process of being steadfast, even when trapped between a rock and a hard place. The experience of faith is a way of being in the world, a way of looking and holding oneself, ever hopeful, ever intimate with God, holding on to covenant when many things physical, psychological, and financial seem to be problematic. At the same time, a faithful countenance will often allow one to be on the offensive and to create proactive strategies so that one is less prone to fall into self-inflicted despair and difficulty. The living of a faithful covenant provides us with a contextual freedom and a will to live responsibly and make good choices, honoring the awesome blessings of God.

Meditation 3

Forgiveness cannot occur without the openness of faith
To transcend vengeance, to embrace deliverance.
To heal wounded hearts, bodies, minds, souls
Wrenched from the intimacy of God's wholeness
By sick folk bent on destruction,
Deluded by their own self-aggrandizement,
Fooled by their own perceptions of reality.

In living the witness of God
Faith overcomes such pathology,
Recreating the innocence and blessed assurance
That accompanied us at birth.
Faith is so amazing, revitalizing, strengthening,

Ever evolving within itself, God, and us,
Creating a cornucopia of blessing.

Faith, an aphrodisiac for pain,
Calms our fears and holds our doubts,
Goes to the very core of our being.
Faith connects us with other
Individuals and communities
Who we dub:
So indifferent, so inferior, so ugly, so prejudiced, so ignorant,
So superior, so righteous, so noble, so intelligent.
Trying to deny them or trying to be like them:
We forgot ourselves; we forgot God.

One of the benefits of living a faithful life is the gift of experiencing forgiveness—to know that God both forgives us and that God will give us the grace to forgive those who have done us wrong. The blessing of forgiveness cannot occur apart from faith. The deliverance that comes with the experience of forgiveness relies on foundational faith. One must believe that God gives the gift of forgiveness and that an individual, with warts and all, can be blessed to experience forgiveness and give that gift to others. As such, forgiveness is essential to healing. Healing happens when one is willing to confess, to name the harm done to him or her or by him or her. After naming this harm one can then express the depths of the accompanying pain, engaging in the healing process. We then ask God to provide the grace to help us move from being continually affected by the pain to transcending the painful situation and the circumstances to moving on to healing and claiming respect and dignity for ourselves. In the process, we come to really see that each of us has value, are significant, and are made in the image of God.

Meditation 4

The eloquence of faith
Provides stability for our shaky personalities
Trapped into what "they said and did";
Defeated by what "they do and have";

> *Impressed by what "they saw and felt."*
> *Faith is the covenant of joy and hope.*
> *Otherwise, the turmoil we perceive in our lives*
> *Makes them threats to our health.*

> *The covenantal power of faith*
> *Reminds us that we are sacred;*
> *Challenges us to change and grow and love;*
> *Excites us to participate with God,*
> *From a place of incarnated generosity.*
> *That covenantal power of faith*
> *Helps us see the abundance,*
> *Helps us give comfort,*
> *Helps us to embrace pain fully,*
> *When our histories have known abuse.*

> *The confessional grace of faith*
> *Gives us the room to grow and change;*
> *Awakens the magnificence of God in us,*
> *Alerts an openness to others so profound*
> *We know we have been changed.*

Faith provides the room for us to make a serious analysis of the past without getting trapped there, helps us assess the present to make room for any correctives, and helps us hear a prophetic voice regarding the future. Faith challenges us and helps us meet the formidable tasks that life brings. In challenging us, faith pushes us to be honest with ourselves about what we feel and think and want. We are pushed to examine our strengths and our weaknesses, particularly noting issues of personal responsibility and accountability. Faith helps us have the courage to face issues that seem almost impossible to comprehend and alter. Faith gives us the energy to believe that by grace we are bigger than our issues and difficulties. Faith nurtures our relationship with God and keeps us excited about our spirituality and our covenant. Faith opens the doors to abundance of spirit with scarcity of resources, and presses us toward the power that comes of unity within community.

Responsive Readings

Responsive Reading 1

Leader: Rejoice for the gifts of faith that sustain us, for the spirituality that integrates us, for the health that lets us move and make a difference in the world.

People: **As people of God we lift our voices in praise and commitment toward being open to other faith communities in love and respect.**

Leader: Rejoice, rejoice, O people of God! Rejoice for the opportunities to share the love of God everywhere you go, to create communties and a world that transcends and embraces the ordinary toward extraordinary love of God.

People: **As children of God we rejoice in the gifts of youth and old age, for each moment is a time for us to be more god-like, walking a pathway toward unity amid difference.**

Leader: Rejoice and give thanks for the community we represent, for our health, strength, vision, and ministries that we are so blessed to serve and to witness.

People: **As children of God we exalt the name of God, the name high over any other name. We pledge to use sweet tongues as we speak and are in communion with those who are different from us.**

Leader: Rejoice and give thanks for the traditions on which we stand, for those we need to reform, as we grow and serve in this present age.

All: **As children of God we embrace this day as a unique day made by God wherein we open ourselves to be blessed and to be a blessing to others.**

In a world that has so many different cultures and peoples and ways of being, it almost seems impossible that we can get

199

along—that the possibility actually exists for us to coexist peacefully. History tells us that we cannot live side by side in peace. Human beings destroy one another: think about the deaths and the destruction in Kosovo and the former Yugoslavia; Rwanda, Ireland, and all of the bombings in the 1990s; the ancient, medieval, romantic, and modern eras' heinous crimes of conquest, genocide, molestation; tortures that occurred in the crusades; the Holocaust; the Middle Passage; the Trail of Tears; and on and on. From a microcosmic perspective, every day the media in the United States reports crimes committed against women and children, against those deemed minority—particularly those labeled *other*. In some ways everyone is *other* when she or he is disconnected from God, as the broken ties with God mean he or she is not totally who they have been created to be. With a greater awareness of self in relationship through faith, one experiences a new kind of power, shaped by love, and a heightened appreciation for life itself. With such appreciation comes the response of praise and thanksgiving.

Responsive Reading 2

Leader: As awesome as the break of day, as romantic as the setting sun, as lovely as a bed of roses, as quiet as the still of night, so is the magnificence of God and the possibility of God's people.

People: **In the newness of today we bless creation by paying attention, by seeing colors, hearing birds, and listening to one another for the voice of God.**

Leader: As awesome as the break of day, as restful as the incoming tides, as rugged as the sides of mountains, as fleeting as falling leaves, so is the presence and mystery of God and the mysteries of life.

People: **We look to see clearly through the fog and the mist of daily schedules that create havoc in our lives, moving toward a place that is better suited for wholeness and joy.**

Leader: In gratitude for this day we give thanks and commit to loving ourselves better that we may not project our guilt and pain on others.

People: As we come into this sanctuary, this consecrated place of God, we stand in covenant with one another, to God's glory and our healing.

Leader: In gratitude for the gift of this day we shout hallelujah! Blessed be the work of our hands, the thoughts of our minds, the energy of our spirits.

All: As we come into this sanctuary, this holy of holies, we come for renewal, for reclaiming our place as God's children, for reconciling grace that we might be whole.

When we continue to compartmentalize our lives we diminish our capacity to learn, grow, be healthy, and have a fully dynamic relationship with God. As human beings we are so complex and integrally interconnected that any time something goes askew in one part of our system, the other part cannot help being affected. Getting in tune with one's sacredness requires attentiveness to health, faith, and spirituality. One needs to be more aware of the workings of God in the splendor of nature. Again, being in present time can never be underestimated. The gift of present time is the gift to live in the moment, in the newness of each day, in gratitude. The centrality of gratitude and thanksgiving becomes a hallmark of a balanced life where we can take responsibility and not always be ready to project our insecurities, illnesses, and inefficiencies on others so that they become our scapegoats. Within this sense of thanksgiving we experience God's holiness in a more profound way, just as we come to see our own sacredness, and begin to create sanctuary for ourselves and others.

Responsive Reading 3

Leader: We love to tell the story of God, our Creator; of Jesus the Christ, as the incarnation of love; and the Holy Spirit, the one who gives us spiritual power.

People: **As spiritual beings we come to share our stories of God's love and salvation for us; we know the pain and the plenty that accompamy our faithful journeys, and desire to have the courage to be true to our call.**

Leader: We love to tell the stories throughout history that speak of God's steadfastness: eternal in scope, brilliant in origins, complex in diversity and versatility.

People: **As spiritual beings we know the power of the unexplainable, the majesty of faithful reconciling of the irreconcilable, the splendidness of grace in doing the undoable.**

Leader: We know the joy of singing the stories in hymns, anthems, gospels, and other tunes that make plain our faith.

People: **As faithful beings we prayfully accept God's call on our lives and commit to living healthy lives where the spiritual is more important than gaining material things.**

Leader: We know the joy of song, prayer, and dance as we praise God in that great communion of the church universal: global, magnificent, growing, loving communities of faith.

All: **As faithful beings we make a joyful noise for the gifts of salvation and the freedom that comes with such grace: freedom to be, to love, to care.**

One favorite pastime for young children is to sit and listen to someone telling them stories. Libraries have weekly children's hour where children gather to hear stories. In homes of balance and love, parents, older siblings, and guardians often put children to sleep by reading them a bedtime story. Our lives are stories. We have been places, met people, learned from them, and taught them things—most often indirectly. Sometimes stories fail to make sense. Other times they are like parables; they teach us a lesson. In searching for a plausible explanation for the tragedies that come about in some living stories, we often have to concede that *we don't know*. We don't know why certain things happen, as Rabbi Kushner has said in his classic text

When Bad Things Happen to Good People. There is grace in saying, "I don't know," and we need not be embarrassed about not knowing. Sometimes it is in the not knowing that we actually come to learn and know. With some of the stories we also learn of the pain of the journey. Some people's stories have expensive components in that they seem to have a great deal of difficulty. Every time we look around these folks seem to be in trouble. Yet, in the middle of these difficulties, it is still important to create a strategy for living that involves health, involves faith, and involves the human body in acts of praise. Our bodies are marvelous sacred vessels that we are called not to be ashamed of, but to love, nurture, develop, and keep well.

Responsive Reading 4

Leader: The good news of a faithful life radiates throughout everything we do, creating a beacon of hope, regenerating our health, and feeding our spirits as we develop lives of balance and well-being.

People: **As joyous beings we hold fast to our faith but wear it as a loose garment to protect us from the desperation that comes of overwhelming doubt.**

Leader: The blessed news of a faithful life permeates our prayers and our deeds, brings illumination to our path, and forges solidarity between us and our neighbors.

People: **As encouraged beings we rejoice for the wisdom that helps us discern the call God has on each of us, as individuals and as communities of faith, which connects us as ten thousand flakes of new fallen snow.**

Leader: The inspiring news of a faithful life revitalizes us and presses us to be all God created us to be, and moves us to confess our shortcomings, to celebrate our strengths, and to seek balance between the two.

People: **As motivated beings we grasp the energy of God that courses through our veins, we sense the brilliance of God that called us into being, we taste the goodness of God that enlightens our own awareness.**

Leader: The resurrecting news of a faithful life reclaims us and challenges us to see and know who we are—a covenant people loved by God.

All: As spirited beings we look with new eyes, hear with new ears, touch with new hands, smell and taste in new ways, formed for the glory of God and for the edification of our sacredness.

A faithful life has an incredible amount of space for belief and doubt. Doubt is often not the enemy; doubt can be a catalyst for attaining renewed, resurrected faith by God's grace. Because such a life has this much room it embodies a kind of illumination that if we but look, the light of faith will at the least get us started on a healthy, helpful path. A faithful life also spares us the insanity of desperation. Desperation repels, it does not attract, whether in a spiritual, business, or academic setting. People do not want to be involved with the kind of pathological neediness that comes with desperation. Some of us have not gotten jobs or not been invited into the inner circles because we sent out messages that stated, "I'm not good enough"; "I'm so desperate I'll do anything to get ahead and will probably do anything poorly." A faithful life helps us stand on the edge of such desolate places and sometimes helps us see beyond the valley and over the hill to a promise of what is to come.

Prayers of Commitment

Prayer of Commitment 1

For all the gifts of faith that God chooses to give us this day, we give thanks. For the times when we forgot God but in faithfulness God did not forget us, we are grateful. In the days of our youth gird us up in faith and hope, that our lives exhibit covenant power and freedom. Let us not ever be torn from You, Gracious One; let us not descend to the bowels of hell because our faith has died. We love You and honor Your witness to us and concern for us. We pray that our faith is alive in every task of ministry to which we set our hands. May the incarnated love of Christ bless the vision for ourselves, our families, and our churches. May we be faithful to these visions and hold all our community members in the highest regard. Let not our hearts be troubled because we feel doubtful or insecure. Let us come to You with these concerns that You might quiet our fears and strengthen our resolve. We pray for a faith that will not shrink, decline, or diminish. We pray for a faith that will sustain, embrace, and guide our path throughout life, for this day, and the next.

In spite of all our intentions, our best planning, and our well-disciplined spiritual and prayer life, there may be times when our faith runs a little thin. Such an encounter may feel like self-betrayal or like we are letting someone down. Just as Jesus cried out from Gethsemane, "My God, My God, why have you forsaken me?" (see Ps. 22), we too may have days when we feel God has abandoned us. One key thing to remember is that God chose to create the world and put human beings in it. God has promised, in various covenants, an undying faithful commitment to us. Just as God chooses us, we can choose God. By choosing God we signify a powerful life-changing relationship and are making a commitment to live out our lives in the context of our love for God. Faith thus becomes a life force that fuels all our relationships, particularly our relationship with God.

Prayer of Commitment 2

Blessed Lord, we cry out to You from the depths of our being, in this hour of need and concern. Though we believe and have committed our lives to You, we feel faint of heart and slow of action. Although we desire to live out our faith, challenges arise every day that seem to make living out faith a major obstacle. Even when we pray it feels like we are merely uttering empty words. When we go to worship it seems that nothing moves or inspires us. In this wilderness of disjointed reality make us whole and shore up our faith. Let our faith be that of the mustard seed, that it may grow into a tree of strong belief. Anoint our eyes, ears, and heart, that we are moved as we prepare to come to worship, that we might fully participate in our adoration of You. Please send us your messengers that we might sense Your presence in more profound ways, knowing that this lull in our faith will pass. We know that You have heard our prayers and our cries, and for this we give thanks.

Bless the faith of our community that the lives we live become a beacon to all, signaling that You are real, that You love us, and that You are still in the healing business.

There are times when we tend to shut down and become numb, either because we are so overwhelmed or because we have gone through a traumatic experience and the only way we know to cope is to shut down completely. A healthier response is to seek counseling, perhaps spiritual direction, and/or do journaling. Writing, prayer, and confession are key components for the process of reconciliation, for coming out from under extreme duress. Sometimes our male counterparts have difficulty in getting to a place of expressing their emotions because when they were infants, barely walking, we made them stop crying. We told them, "You are a man!" How can a male child be a man at two years of age? What kind of hoax do we daily perpetrate when insisting our male children must be men, that they cannot cry because that makes them wimps? Where then does all of their rage go? The rage, the sense of denial and betrayal, moves from thought process to paralysis, possibly to a deep sense of loss and emptiness. The male child on the other end of this rage feels violated and left out, needing always to prove he is a man. The female child is often given a similar bill of goods in the reverse: lots of tears will get you where you want to go in life. A faithful model for these extremes is balance that comes of knowing how and where to express our deepest feelings, of being able to process these thoughts and feelings without beating up on ourselves for having them, and learning to embrace the experience.

Prayer of Commitment 3

Mother/Father of all, help us make sense out of the confusion in our minds and our lives. Building on faith, we know that You care for us and that we can approach You in simplicity and love. Bless our faith, that we might have a stronger trust in You and know when we have heard Your desire for our hearts. In Your own way and in Your own time, bless us to clarify the priorities in our lives. As we work more and more hours we seem to have less and less: less time and less financial resources. Give us a sense of wisdom so that we may be good stewards of our human and financial resources, in concert with our call to be persons of faith. Help us be good stewards of our time and the time of others. O God, we often trust You for religious and spiritual issues but not for all aspects of our lives. Help us be open to Your grace and mercy in all our being and all our doing. As people of the covenant, send Your clouds by day and Your pillars of fire by night to be our guides. May the words that we speak be faithful; may the prayers and meditations that we offer from our minds and our hearts ever rest on your covenant faith that empowers us to endure.

None of us have to know everything in the world to make it, but it certainly helps if we know how to read. In countless instances trouble emerges because someone misread or did not read carefully. Reading can help stem the tide of confusion. As we read, we see and listen to many people's stories. We learn that we are not alone. So many wonderful venues open to us when we read. We can bless our faith lives by reading sacred texts and works of inspiration to help us deal with the rocky times and celebrate the good times. Reading these texts and thinking critically about how we interpret them and the subsequent implications for our lives are major concerns. In the process of thinking critically and getting clearer and clearer about faith, we learn to be good stewards of our human and financial resources. At a place of faith we can leave the quagmire of greed and desperation to move to a place of generosity and abundance.

Prayer of Commitment 4

God of health and life, we bless You for Your marvelous works within the human body. You have been so faithful in Your creation that much of what we do comes by training and reflex. We give thanks for the magnificent construction of our bodies, for the wonderful creativity of our minds, and for the ability to live a faithful life of spirituality, using our bodies, minds, and souls. For this we know gratitude unspeakable. Bless us that we respect ourselves so that we see taking care of ourselves as a central component of faith. Let us not take any of our gifts and graces for granted. Help us see the sacramental connection between our faith and health as funda-

> *mental components of our spirituality. Bless our caregivers, health practitioners, pastors, ministers, and spiritual directors that they might be loving and proficient in designing our care. Help them use a vocabulary that is meaningful and clear in their diagnostic work. Help us hear with faithful, discerning ears that we might be able to interpret their words to fit our case. Bless us all and make us one body of the faithful, who clearly understand our lives in light of Your call.*

The faithful life is a refreshing pilgrimage: one journeys to many places but returns always to her or his Center for perspective and insight. Not only is God the Center, but God stands as a lightning rod to counter the damage that can be done to various human internal and communal systems. To lead a faith-filled life is to know the meaning of hard work. Just as construction workers toil all day in often inclement weather, children of faith must be open to God's grace to afford multiple faith encounters along with the study of scripture and other spiritual works to achieve that place of peace and serenity. Peace and serenity do not become passive hideouts but active vehicles for expressing divine compassion. In this kind of environment everyone learns to respect one another and we learn not to take people or God's grace for granted. This grace affords healing, learning, and loving.

---

1. Botterweck, G. Johannes, and Helmer Ringgren, eds. *Theological Dictionary of the Old Testament*, vol. 5 (Grand Rapids: Eerdmans, 1986), 431-32.

2. Kittel, Gerard, ed., *Theological Dictionary of the New Testament*, vol. 9 (Grand Rapids: Eerdmans, 1974), 411.

3. Ibid., 413.